Job Analysis
at the Speed of Reality

Darin E. Hartley

HRD Press • Amherst • Massachusetts

Published by: HRD Press, Inc.
22 Amherst Road
Amherst, MA 01002
(800) 822-2801 (U.S. and Canada)
(413) 253-3488
(413) 253-3490 (Fax)
http://www.hrdpress.com

First Edition, First Printing

ISBN 0-87425-487-6

Typesetting by Michele Anctil
Cover design by Eileen Klockars
Editorial work by Suzanne Bay
Cartoons by Cody Stromberg

Table of Contents

Preface

In January of 1996, as a new Dell employee, I was asked to perform several job analyses for sales positions. I had moved from a full time position at Lockheed Martin, where I conducted many three-day sessions in job analysis, and I was feeling confident—even a little arrogant—because I knew that when it came to job analysis, three days was considered a relatively short period of time. Some job analyses can take months to complete.

My boss, however, wasn't as impressed as I expected her to be. In fact, my feelings were a little hurt when my request for subject matter experts (SMEs) was met with an eruption of laughter. There was just no way a high-powered sales organization was going to allow people to be away from their selling environments for three whole days. I knew then that I had to virtually reinvent the job analysis process and devise a newer, more direct method of collecting data about job tasks and responsibilities. And I needed to adapt the process quickly if I was going to use it in this new environment. I needed a leaner, swifter, more straightforward methodology that would give me enough information to start building worthwhile training for the incumbents. I needed some way to perform the analysis that was relatively painless, that added something significant to the educational planning process, and that didn't interfere with business. I was confident that organizations like Dell would welcome a leaner and swifter process.

Job Analysis at the Speed of Reality details a streamlined, business-oriented method that is sound enough to be used to create valid task lists, which can then be used as a basis for performance-based behavioral change. It is written for trainers, managers, human performance technologists, consultants, and other industry professionals, but the information will not make everyone comfortable because we ask them to give up some of their traditional power. However, this apparent loss is more than offset by the enhanced credibility and stronger client relationships that will be gained from a process that is faster and that produces better results. In fact, letting the participants feel like they are important to the job analysis process (which they are) and "owners" of the content will have advantages later on when it comes to training and development.

There are other benefits to this new process. Job Analysis at the Speed of Reality will allow you to:

- Gather job data quickly (normally two to three hours)

- Make job-based training recommendations rapidly

- Save money on costly consultants

- Use a consistent and repeatable process throughout the organization

- Create validated task lists that can be used in a variety of ways.

The book is divided into two parts:

Part One includes the theory of job analysis, a comparison of traditional methods, and what others have to say about job analyses that were less than successful. A complete description of the JASR method follows, breaking the process down into easy-to-follow steps accompanied by facilitation tips and information about products and uses. Part Two is the Field Book, which contains facilitator, resource, and Internet guides, templates, a materials checklist, a glossary of terms and list of acronyms, references, and the all-important sample task lists that will help you develop yours.

The development of this process grew out of a reawakening I experienced in recent years. I have learned to view the process as a two-way one in which the participants and the facilitator *help one another;* I allow job incumbents to tell me what they need to know and how and when they need to know it. I ask direct questions that aren't littered with training jargon and performance-isms, and in return I get succinct operational task statements. It is my hope that you immerse yourself in the first half of this book and then run out and find a group of people in need of a job analysis so that you can conduct it quickly and efficiently—before lunch.

Acknowledgements

There are many people whom I feel obligated and delighted to acknowledge. First and foremost, I must thank my loving and supportive wife, Libbie. She believed in me enough to take a chance on a first date with me, and she continues to believe in and cheer for me louder than anyone else. I'd also like to thank my parents, Bill Hartley and Kristi Lindley, and my other parents, Harley and Mary Eddy, for voluminous love and encouragement. Three professors at Idaho State University, Dr. John Bobbell, Dr. Chuck Humphrey, and Dr. Robert Croker, supported my academic achievements and kept me excited about the field of training and performance improvement at the undergraduate and graduate levels. David Jedrziewski, a mentor-and-boss and now mentor-and-fellow-Dell employee, has delivered sage training and writing advice over the years. John Cone´, President of Dell Computer Corporation's Dell University, mentally challenges me on a regular basis to keep our organization as efficient as it can be. Jack Tootson, formerly the Director of IAMS University, has joined Dell and been an able mentor and good friend as well. Dr. Ferdinand Tesoro of Dell provided me with information and tips on the publishing process, and referred me to Barry Davis at HRD Press. Barry, who believed in me enough to give me the opportunity to pen this for you, was ably replaced by Chris Hunter with no glitches. Cody Stromberg is the brilliant artist who provided the thematic and fun artwork for this book. Ed Metz provided an excellent initial read of the manuscript and offered super suggestions to improve the readability of the book.

I'd also like to thank the hundreds of unnamed participants who have provided me with some of the richest learning experiences I've ever had. Not only did I get to meet new people with each session, but I also got to learn about *the business:* I learned how people interact and with whom they interact, and I learned something about organizational politics. I also discovered that you can always learn something to make you better at what you do.

Chapter 1
Job Analysis Nightmares

A job analysis is a systematic process for collecting and analyzing information about jobs. It provides information about such things as the work environment, the work performed, work relationships, and basic training requirements. It can be conducted in a variety of ways and generally results in a validated list of tasks and responsibilities for the position.

Before you learn about Job Analysis at the Speed of Reality (JASR), we need to review some examples of job analysis gone awry. Many well-intentioned and expensive attempts to analyze jobs have been made over the years that have turned out to be ineffective and sometimes even detrimental to an organization's effort to improve performance.

The job analysis stories have come from diverse sources. I called peers, consultants, and training managers and asked them to share some of their worst experiences with job analysis. I also sent queries to a couple of listservs, including the Training and Development Listserv (TRDEV-L) and the Job Analysis Listserv. (Information on listservs can be found in the Field Book under Job Analysis Internet Resources.) I asked these people to share with me the best of the worst job analysis stories they had heard about or experienced, and they responded enthusiastically. I'll share several of those experiences with you now, so you can get a sense of what is happening out there.

MIAs—Missing In Analysis

Fred Nickols, a human performance consultant, shared this story:

"Many years ago, a very large telecommunications firm spent many millions of dollars conducting a job analysis of first-level and second-level supervisors. When it was completed, the analysis filled sixteen 3-inch 3-ring binders."

"One of the findings of this job analysis was that the first- and second-level supervisors' writing skills were seriously deficient. Accordingly, the company spent $7,000,000 on a writing course through which passed thousands of first- and second-level managers."

"Consistent with sound professional practice, a follow-up study was conducted to determine the degree of improvement. To the human resources department's horror, the results indicated that matters were actually worse than before."

Fred continued his story. "I was asked to look into the matter. After reviewing key information sources, this is what I reported. 'You HR folks overlooked a key analysis question. Your job study was conducted by asking third-level managers to rate the writing skills of the first- and second-level managers. The third-level managers said the writing skills of the first- and second-level managers were lousy. So, you went out and spent millions of dollars on a professional writing course. Now the first- and second-level managers write the way they've been taught to do. Of course the third-level managers are going to say matters are worse; in fact, they probably are.'"

"You failed to ask the obvious question: What is it that first- and second-level managers write that third-level managers see and are in a position to judge? The answer is correspondence, memos, and other documents prepared for the third-level manager's signature. When the third-level managers told you that the first- and second-level managers couldn't write, they were really saying that the first- and second-level managers couldn't draft stuff the third-level managers were comfortable signing."

"Now, you and I know that there's hardly any consistency among the third-level managers' writing preferences. So, any real solution to the writing skills deficiency problem wasn't going to take the form of an off-the-shelf writing course. Instead, it should have taken the form of helping the first- and second-level managers figure out their particular boss's preferences and how to satisfy them. This could have involved talking with the administrative assistant, reviewing the files to see what had been signed and what had been rejected or rewritten, and even scheduling a session with the boss to review some writing samples. But in no case was a commercial writing skills package going to address the requirements of the third-level managers."

"Millions of dollars were spent on the job study and the wrong training solution."

Lessons Learned

The example cited above illustrates how you can spend excessive amounts of money and create mounds of documentation and still not improve performance in the least, if the appropriate people are not consulted during the job analysis process. The most appropriate people to consult in this scenario were missing in the analysis.

"The Expensive Consultant is Better" Trap

A. L. Brockwell e-mailed the following job analysis story to me.

"A global advertising agency has not updated job descriptions in its flagship headquarters office since the late 1980s–early 1990s. Two years ago (1996), the corporate training and development office, which is the designated repository of job descriptions and is deluged with requests from around the world for those descriptions, decided to put the matter to rest by proposing:

1. A corporate-wide standards format for job descriptions.

2. A Lotus Notes™ database for storing job descriptions, providing access to anyone in the world who needs them for whatever reason.

3. A guide to walk managers through the process of developing job descriptions and entering them into the database (with expert consultation if necessary).

4. Completed job descriptions of the 30 "key" jobs in the company.

    The total cost: $12,000.

    Result: Funds DENIED.

Now the company is paying an external consulting firm bundles of money to develop a job evaluation scheme. Critical to that effort is—of course—valid job descriptions. Therefore, the consultants are now devising the job description guide at many times what it would have cost just two years ago."

Lessons Learned

This story clearly shows that some organizations fear simplifying their processes: There *is no way you could be done with that job! You got it done too quickly. Go redo it!*

It's true. Management gets very wary of work processes that are perceived as being too easy. Some organizations believe that there is not enough company expertise in job analysis to conduct it internally. This fear of analyzing job scopes and responsibilities is an expensive one that often leads to a dependence on outside consultants.

Hamster Wheel Job Analysis

When I got out of the U.S. Navy years ago, one of the first jobs I got was as a training analyst/developer at a vitrification facility in the southeastern United States. A vitrification facility is a special plant that takes liquid nuclear waste and converts it to a solid glass body so that the waste is in a more stable chemical state. The facility was under construction and many of the staff positions were being analyzed. The difficulty with this situation was that it took nine to twelve months to complete the job analysis for one of the operator positions. So, by the time the analysis was completed on a position, new systems were in place at the facility; new interactions and job responsibilities invalidated much of the initial analysis work. The training analysts found themselves in a state of perpetual analysis: Like hamsters on the hamster wheel, they were working hard, but getting nowhere.

This was detrimental to the development of curriculum and instruction programs, since it took so long to get the analysis completed. The process held up training and development not just for new hires, but for current staff members. The costs to the company in terms of lost opportunity were immense.

Lessons Learned

When an organization is trying to create developmental materials and support systems based on job analysis, it is imperative that the analysis be completed as quickly as possible. Each passing day that a job analysis is put off tends to invalidate the current study. If an analysis is completed efficiently in a short period of time, interventions can be created quickly to support workforce development.

What's the Half-Life of a Job Analysis?

One individual I spoke with relayed a story about a Fortune 500™ company that hadn't conducted any job analyses since 1983. Twelve years later, the company decided on a reduction in force and used the analyses conducted back in 1983 as the basis for termination decisions. As a consequence, many people were fired because of information that was more than a decade old. Jobs change and evolve on a daily basis, and today's work environments are dynamic and fluid. Political, fiscal, and/or social issues can rattle an organization if it is not prepared. For these reasons, it is important to have a job analysis methodology at the ready so that positions can be examined as soon as a company's critical business situation changes.

Lessons Learned

This company unknowingly put itself at significant legal and financial risk (multi-million dollar risks) had these job cuts been challenged in court. Because of the dynamic nature of jobs, work environments, organizations, and organizational politics, job analyses should be scheduled on a regular basis so that job requirements are accurate and up-to-date. At no time should a hiring or firing decision be made on out-of-date job analysis data. The half-life of job analyses is *not indefinite*.

Summary

The aforementioned examples have addressed the repercussions of over-analyzing jobs, under-analyzing jobs, using the wrong people to conduct analyses, using improper methods, and using outdated job analyses to make critical staffing and personnel decisions. The JASR method is quick, efficient, consistent, and repeatable, and uses checks and balances to make certain that the most appropriate people take part in the job analysis session. This Speed of Reality method of job analysis would have minimized the nightmares described in this chapter. Now that you've seen the kinds of problems that come up when job analyses are conducted improperly or not at all, perhaps you will begin to see the powerful advantages of the Job Analysis at the Speed of Reality method.

Chapter 2
An Overview of Job Analysis
at the Speed of Reality

Introduction

The human performance improvement industry uses job analysis to make sure training and development activities are focused and effective. There's only one problem. Traditional methods of analysis can be laborious and time consuming. In this day and age when line management is asking tough questions about the validity of training, as well as the expense, it can be very difficult to justify the need for a comprehensive job analysis. And, as we said before, there is always a tendency on the part of management to overanalyze some jobs and underanalyze others.

Since time is money in the world of business, instructional systems designers, training specialists, training managers, training directors, staffing specialists, managers, and human performance consultants must continue to streamline processes. Simultaneously, we must begin to gather any information that we consider relevant to the job analysis.

Job Analysis Methods

Traditional job analysis methods include the following: one-on-one interviewing; behavioral event interviews; phone interviews; surveys; work assessments; Developing a Curriculum (DACUM); job analysis worksheets; observations; and procedural review. All of these methods, which will be discussed in more detail in the next chapter, can be used to gather information for a job analysis. However, most are very tedious and cumbersome. The DACUM process conceived in the late 1960s is generally viewed as the quickest method used today, but it can still take two to three days to obtain a validated task list.

The measure of a sound job analysis is a valid task list. This list consists of the functional or duty areas for a position, the related tasks, and basic training recommendations. Subject matter experts (SMEs) and supervisors for the position being analyzed should validate the final list.

Job Analysis at the Speed of Reality

The Job Analysis at the Speed of Reality (JASR) method is a tested process that helps analysts complete a job analysis of a typical job in two to three hours and then deliver a validated task list. The JASR process can be used to create a validated task list with a group of subject matter experts and managers in 2–3 hours. The author has used the JASR method approximately 25 times in the past several years, each time quickly and successfully creating usable task lists that are at a consistent level with analyses using DACUM-like methods.

JASR Principles

The JASR process is based on the following four principles:

1. Job incumbents (exemplars) should know their jobs better than anyone else. They can provide accurate, timely content information about the job.

2. JASR participants want to spend a minimum amount of time providing job data during a session and business leadership wants to minimize disruption to business operations.

3. Since JASR participants don't spend as much time thinking about "training" as training professionals do, they don't require much "orientation" to the process.

4. JASR uses the quickest methods and best possible technology to complete the job analysis.

Minimizing Orientation of the Participants

The third principle is a key difference between JASR and the DACUM and DACUM-like processes. In the DACUM process, the facilitator can spend as much as 25% of the time orienting participants, explaining the process, and defining training terminology like *job* and *duty area*. Identifying task statements and how they are conceived, etc., takes more time. The hard truth is that people who don't train or deal with human resource issues just don't think about training as much as we do. Most workers don't sit around on the job and think, "Hmmm . . . I wonder what duty area I'll be working in today?" or "I can't go do what the boss asked, because she didn't formulate the task statement properly." When we as training and performance professionals realize this tenet, it frees us up to jump right into job analysis with our JASR participants. Most job incumbents can readily tell you what they do and what they need to be able to do on the job without fully understanding what a *duty area* or *functional area* is. Evidence to this effect has been gathered from many such sessions conducted by the author in the past several years.

Gaining Efficiencies

The fourth principle is also important, since we want to be as efficient as we can when we conduct these kinds of sessions. The DACUM methodology and other related job analysis methods recommend the use of storyboards to complete some of the steps in the process: Each task statement must be written on an 8½ × 11-inch piece of paper and posted on the wall near its corresponding duty area. These task statements are then revised and possibly reordered during this step. This transcribing and paper-juggling consumes considerable time in the process. The JASR facilitator is more efficient, transferring information to one flip chart and using different colors and symbols to manipulate the information on one page. Post-it™ notes also help, and it is even possible to use collaborative online tools to conduct these sessions. (See Chapter 7.)

JASR Roles

Several key players are integral to the success of the JASR sessions.

A **skillful facilitator** is key to any JASR session's success. The facilitator is an expert in the job analysis process; he or she must be able to make presentations, lead discussions, ask probing questions, guide participants, and focus the session. The facilitator is often responsible for setting up the session, as well.

Another key player is the **recorder.** The recorder uses a computer during the session (usually a laptop) to key in responses in real time, while session participants are interacting. In this way, the participants can readily sign the task list at the end of the session. The recorder should be familiar with the process and be able to manipulate word processing templates, and can also act as a timekeeper.

Job incumbents and **managers** are also very important to this process, since they provide the content. The facilitator should periodically remind this group of the immense value they contribute to the process. Generally speaking, there should be four to six job incumbents (exemplars), as well as a supervisor and a manger for each position.

Materials and Equipment

Certain materials and other resources are required: A room with tables should be reserved in advance of the meeting, outfitted with the following supplies and equipment:

- Two flip chart stands
- Several pads of flip chart paper (self-sticking pads are best)
- Name tents
- Water-based markers (an assortment of colors)
- Portable computer
- Blank disks
- Access to a printer
- Blank scratch paper for participants
- Pencils or pens.

These should be assembled ahead of time. If you conduct these sessions on a regular basis, consider putting together a " JASR Kit"—a mobile kit that contains all of the tools needed to conduct a JASR session, such as name tents, scratch paper, water-based markers, pre-fabricated slides, a facilitator guide, and sample task lists.

Room Setup

Set up the room as follows:

- Arrange the tables in a "U" shape so participants can converse easily with each other.

- Place a name tent, scrap paper, a colored marker, and a pencil or pen at each seat.

- Set up both flip chart stands with pads in the front of the room.

- Set up the recorder's portable computer where he or she can see the information that is generated and hear the dialogue between the facilitator and participants.

The facilitator can now start the session.

JASR Steps

There are only a few key steps in the JASR process. The key steps are:

1. Greet the participants and conduct introductions.

2. Briefly explain the JASR process and why they are part of it. Discuss the role of content expert.

3. Determine the scope of the job to be analyzed and establish parameters for the analysis—what is and what isn't going to be analyzed.

4. Identify functional areas or duty areas for the job.

5. Identify tasks within each duty area and state whether they require formal training or non-formal training.

6, Print the task list and have it signed by the group.

The steps will be discussed in more detail in Chapter 4.

Facilitation Techniques

The facilitator makes the JASR process easier by using several techniques. *Brainstorming* is one of the most important; the facilitator should be able to brainstorm with a group of individuals. A *modified nominal group technique* is also used. When a question is posed to the group, the participants have a chance to write responses on scratch paper. They are then called upon in an orderly fashion around the table to provide input. As each participant provides input, he or she strikes the response from his or her list (as do the other participants) and the next participant answers. This continues until all participants have exhausted their lists.

At the end of the process, a validated task list is created. It consists of a job name (or title) for the analysis, a listing of duty areas, the tasks, the training level, and the signatures of the participants.

Task List Uses

There are several ways to use a validated task list, which is a list that hierarchically breaks a job down into its component duty or functional areas and tasks. The task list is validated because exemplar job incumbents and managers are involved in the process.

- *Curriculum* can be developed based on the skill and knowledge areas of the position that were identified from the task list. Learning objectives can be written from the task analysis and this provides the basis for any curriculum.

- The task list can be used as a basis for *hiring personnel*. Because the information from the task list specifies the major requirements of the job, staffing personnel can use this as the basis for behavioral interview guides.

- Individuals can use the task lists as *self-assessment tools* for professional development. A person can look at the task list and identify areas for improvement. See a sample of self-assessment in Chapter 7.

- Managers can use the task lists as a basis for *performance planning and management*. A manager can look at the task list and create developmental goals for his or her direct reports.

- The task lists can also be used in *organizational planning*. If a manager creates a matrix with his or her personnel as well as the task list, he or she can quickly see where there are gaps in the organization. The manager can use this information to help round out the organization (i.e., assess the overall competence of the organization and make complementary hiring decisions).

Sample products and methods of creating them will be discussed in Chapter 5.

Comparative Results

Are results comparable with other methods? The answer is a resounding "yes." The author has conducted many job analyses using traditional methods; the task lists created with the JASR method are comparable to the task lists created by traditional methods, including the DACUM. Both methods generate about the same number of duty areas, task statements, and level of tasks. The Department of Energy used a similar process at a high-hazard nuclear tritium facility and saved over $1 million by *not* using a traditional job analysis approach.

Learning JASR

With practice, most people can learn how to facilitate this process. The author recommends that those who wish to learn the process observe JASR facilitators. If you have good facilitation skills and know how to group tasks into duty areas, then you can facilitate these sessions.

JASR's Future

Collaborative working sessions like JASR show future promise, particularly considering the abundant technology that exists today. (See Chapter 7.) Collaboration and "chat" tools make it possible now to facilitate sessions in real time—with people in multiple physical locations. This tremendous breakthrough alleviates some of the traditional problems associated with working with remote groups.

Summary

In summary, the JASR method for job analysis is a reliable, proven method to quickly create validated task lists. The end product, which can be used for many purposes, is the basis for many potential training and staffing interventions. So, the next time you're asked to conduct a job analysis, don't cringe; you can conduct job analysis at the speed of reality and positively affect your business's bottom line.

In the next chapter, we will provide an overview of the many methods available for job analysis. Each description will include advantages and disadvantages you should consider prior to your next job analysis session(s).

Chapter 3
A Review of Job Analysis Methods
(Including Advantages and Disadvantages)

The Job Analysis at the Speed of Reality (JASR) method is not the only way to conduct job analyses. In some cases, you might want to use the JASR method in tandem with some of the techniques that will be discussed in this chapter. There are advantages and disadvantages to every analysis method you may want to use; assess your situation well when you prepare to conduct the job analysis to collect the most relevant data. There are some situations where a more rigorous analysis is appropriate, but for most job analyses, the JASR method will help you create the all-important validated task list on which you can base other products, such as behavioral interview guides, training, performance planning, etc.

DACUM

The DACUM method, which has been around since the early 1960s, takes a structured focus group or "tabletop" approach to create the validated task list, using a group of exemplars and managers. It is an eight-step process that uses nominal group technique and storyboarding, along with subject matter experts, to create the validated task list. We call it a "validated" list because the subject matter experts and mid- and senior-level managers are involved in the entire process. The task list is generated in real time on the second or third day of the DACUM session and must be signed by all participants in the room. This streamlines the review and approval process and allows training personnel to start task analysis and content development quickly. DACUM has been the basis for many of the currently popular tabletop approaches. Let's look at some of the advantages and disadvantages of this method.

DACUM Method	
Advantages	**Disadvantages**
Quick—Generally can be done in three days.	*Cumbersome*—The storyboarding and listing of individual tasks on pieces of paper can take a long time to do.
Self-validating—Exemplars in the job, supervisor(s), and manager(s) take part in the sessions at the same time, so each group can cross-check the other.	*Orientation is too long*—The group can spend close to 25% of the job analysis session learning training and job analysis terminology prior to the actual job analysis session.
Proven methodology—This technique has been used for over thirty years to conduct job analysis.	*Need DACUM Certification*—To legally conduct a DACUM session, the organization must obtain certification from the DACUM licensees at the Center on Education and Training for Employment.
Ownership-instilled—Since job incumbents and managers are used to create their own organization's task lists to be used for training and professional development, these people feel like they actually "own" the analysis process and any subsequent training development. It alleviates the misconception that training is built around the whims of the training department.	

Behavioral Event Interviews (BEIs)

David McClelland created an interviewing technique to identify the competencies of average and superior performers. His technique was based on a similar method known as *critical incident technique:* Trained facilitators ask a series of structured questions of job incumbents to determine the similarities of average performers and superior performers. The Behavioral Event Interview process asks a subject to describe three peak successes and three major failures in short-story fashion. The interviewer acts as an investigative reporter, asking the following questions: What led up to the situation? Who was involved? What did you think about, feel, and want to accomplish in dealing with the situation? What did you actually do? What happened? What was the outcome of the incident? (Spencer, p. 5) Several sets of interviews are conducted for each position in order to collect the necessary data.

Some advantages and disadvantages of this method are listed below.

Behavioral Event Interview Method	
Advantages	**Disadvantages**
Provides insight into personality traits and other characteristics required to do the job—Job analysis focuses on identifying the major elements of the job. These interviews are used to identify the traits of average and superior performers.	*Can be slow*—The logistics and potential time it takes to conduct a series of interviews can be daunting. The average interview takes about one day to conduct, analyze, and transcribe. If you multiply this by the number of one-on-one interviews that are conducted, the time disappears even quicker.
Specific data is generated for assessment, training, and organizational planning—This method provides specific and detailed information about effective and ineffective job behaviors. The method also provides the training developer with a wealth of actual case studies and events that can be used for future training development projects.	*Method requires specialized training*—Not everybody can use this method. There are subtleties and steps that must be learned in the process with experience and/or coaching.
	Inefficient method—Several interviews may be needed to collect all the necessary information. This method is not a practical one for a large number of jobs.
	Can be costly—Travel and related costs can be prohibitive if interviews are scheduled in multiple locations. Job analyst labor costs can also be high with this method.
	Method can miss less-obvious tasks—This method focuses on critical incidents, so it is very easy to miss some of the more *common* tasks that are still important to the job incumbent on a daily basis.

Observation

One of the most obvious ways you can learn about how someone in a job performs tasks associated with the job is to observe job incumbents in their work setting. The observer notes tasks performed, steps of major tasks, tools and equipment used, communication processes, procedures and references used, interactions with other personnel, administrative activities, etc. The observer can also ask questions of those personnel being observed. For positions such as phone sales representatives and customer service representatives, monitoring incoming and outgoing calls can be a good way to "observe." It is recommended that job analysts observe the exemplar incumbents to make sure the completed task list will represent top job performance.

Some advantages and disadvantages of the observation method are listed below.

Observation Method	
Advantages	**Disadvantages**
Ideal for gathering information about manual tasks—For job incumbents on manufacturing floors or in other positions where repetitive (or prefigured work) is conducted, observations are a great way to collect information.	*Can be slow*—The logistics and potential time it takes to conduct a series of observations about job performance or tasks can be daunting. To make matters worse, most people do not complete all the tasks they are responsible for in a single day.
	The right personnel must be chosen for observation—Job incumbents who are completing tasks incorrectly or in an unsafe manner can taint the job analysis results.
	Inefficient method—It can take many visits and observations to develop an appropriate task list, and several people will have to be involved.
	Can be costly—Travel and related costs can be prohibitive if interviews or observations have to be scheduled in multiple locations. Job analyst labor costs can also be expensive with this method.
	Difficult to use for "knowledge workers"—Many people do not perform manual tasks in their jobs; observing what occurs in people's heads is impossible.

Procedural Review

You can gather a tremendous amount of information about a person's job by reviewing the work and administrative procedures associated with that position. Major duty or functional areas are likely to already be divided up within well-written procedures. The analyst can get groupings of tasks and task statements right from the procedures that he or she is reviewing. A major drawback with this method, however, is that many current positions do not have well documented procedures in place. This is especially true in the case of knowledge workers. How would you write a step-by-step procedure for creative problem solving?

Interviews

An interview is a powerful tool that can be used to gather information from job incumbents and managers about job requirements. The interview technique can be adapted to either a flexible or a highly structured format.

Here are some tips:

- Before conducting any interview, you should determine who the key interviewees are for the information you seek.

- Create a list of questions that you will ask the interviewees.

- Conduct the interviews and record the information as you get it. A form you create in advance and a portable tape recorder work well. (Make sure that the person you are interviewing agrees to your taping the interview.)

- As soon as possible after the interview, summarize the questions you asked with corresponding answers and submit this to the interviewee for verification and revision if necessary.

Some of the advantages and disadvantages of the interview method are listed on the chart that follows.

Interview Method	
Advantages	**Disadvantages**
Specific Information can be gathered—The interviewer can gather very specific information from the interview.	*Can be slow*—The logistics and potential time it takes to conduct a series of interviews to gather job information can be daunting.
Allows probing and clarification—Information that an analyst obtains from a survey is relatively straightforward. Once the survey is submitted, however, it is hard to get back to the person who submitted it to clarify responses. Conversely, when interviewing a person, the interviewer can "dig down" and get very specific information.	*There is no immediate validation or cross-checking (Minimal synergy)*—Since these interviews are taking place one-on-one, job incumbents and management are not able to "temper" each other's remarks.
	Inefficient method—Because the interviewer will spend much time explaining the purpose of the interview process and providing background information, it is not an efficient use of time. Each interview will have to start the same way.
	Can be costly—For interviews that must be conducted in multiple locations, travel and related costs can be prohibitive.

Surveys

Surveys are tools that can be used to simultaneously gather information from a large cross-section of people. Surveys consist of a set of open- and closed-ended questions that help determine the nature of a job. A variety of media can be used to gather the relevant information: paper surveys, electronic phone surveys, Internet surveys, scanner forms, computer-based disk questionnaires, etc. Care must be taken when writing the survey and also in determining the appropriate target audience and sample size. Also, the kind of survey and number that are distributed will affect the amount of time it takes to compile the responses. Manual input will generally require some form of manual output.

Some advantages and disadvantages of the survey method are listed on the chart that follows.

Survey Method	
Advantages	**Disadvantages**
Large Distribution—The analyst can distribute large numbers of surveys to people as necessary.	*Can be costly*—For surveys that must be conducted in multiple locations, creation, distribution, and compilation of analysis data can be prohibitive.
	Difficult to develop—Because of the self-directed nature of most surveys, it is critical that the surveys have explicit instructions, include appropriate demographic information, and ask questions to get answers that are needed.
	Difficult to compile—If survey data is collected and analyzed manually, this can be a cumbersome process.

The information in this chapter should help you compare the JASR method with methods that have traditionally been used to conduct job analyses. Labor expenses, instrument development costs, and inefficiencies drive up the costs of many of these techniques. The JASR method is a proven business-friendly way to get job information from a group of job incumbents in a short amount of time at a consistent level. The method is explained in detail in the next chapter.

Chapter 4
The JASR Method:
So, How Can I Create a
Valid Task List in Three Hours?

Stan Davis and Christopher Meyer addressed the issue of speed in their book *Blur*. We are all being asked to do more with less all of the time. The authors explain it like this: "Speed is the foreshortening of product life cycles from years to months or even weeks. And Speed is the worldwide electronic network over which financial institutions transfer money at the rate of $41 billion a minute. For the individual, Speed is scores of messages a day, creating near continuous communication. Miss a day and your world moves on without you. Accelerated product life cycles and time-based competition have become part of the business lingo. These experiences change people's perceptions. We now expect real-time responsiveness, 24 hours of every day of the year. This premium placed on anytime, real-time responsiveness is just one example of the growing importance of intangible value." (Davis and Meyer, p. 10–11)

The speed at which we are all operating and the shortened product life cycles both have huge implications for those of us in the training, management, and performance-improvement business. We no longer can linger and study and think and rethink about analyses we conduct. If we wait too long, the job or products or technology will have changed and evolved so much that we will be wasting large amounts of time spinning our wheels in search of the perfect analysis. Its better to think of the analyses and the resultant training and interventions as disposable! The JASR methodology helps us address the question of efficiency, because minimal time is spent on the job analysis process. If the job changes radically in six months, an analyst can validate the analysis quickly with JASR and make any necessary corrections as a result.

In *Mastering the Instructional Design Process* (Rothwell, Kazana, p. 385), the authors posed the following survey question to a group of instructional designers, performance technologists, and organizational development specialists: "How influential are various workplace, workforce, and instructional design field trends to the work of instructional designers?" The top six responses were: 1) technological change, 2) change, 3) cost control orientation, 4) demand for increasing speed in instructional design, 5) increasing importance of knowledge capital, and 6) speed in market change. As you can see, training developers and other change agents are experiencing more pressure to get things done more quickly (and more cost effectively) because of rapidly changing work and technological environments.

This chapter will break down the JASR process into three major areas: Pre-Session Activities, JASR Session Activities, and Post-Session Activities.

Pre-Session Activities

Planning is a key factor in the ultimate success of any session or event that involves logistical arrangements and professionals in an organization. The better the up-front planning, the better the session will be. Getting 6–8 busy people together at the same time for even a two- or three-hour block of time can be frustrating. Here are five key pre-session activities to help you plan:

1. Research the Position

Research the position(s) to be analyzed in the job analysis session. If a job description already exists, study it. Scope the job to see what types of activities and other requirements are associated with the job. Are there requisite skills that are required for the position? Are there similar jobs out there that have already been analyzed? If so, review them. Get familiar with the types of equipment, components, software, and customers that the individuals serve. Do some further digging and research the organizational and political environment if you can. For example, how is the organization structured? What groups in the company interact with the organization in question? Are there political or operational issues that one must know about when talking to people in this position? Locate a glossary of terminology and acronyms used by the organization. The use of job-focused terminology immediately increases the facilitator's credibility with the group. (This is especially important if you are an internal consultant.) Your research will prove that you care enough about the facilitator role to learn everything you can in order to open the communication channels as wide as possible.

2. Identify Subject Matter Experts

Determine who the subject matter experts are for the job you are going to analyze. If you can locate a couple of managers in the position, you are likely to get the names of at least a couple of workers whose work is outstanding. Another useful and powerful technique is to speak with a few job incumbents on the phone or in a face-to-face meeting. Pose the following question: "When you have questions or aren't sure about the way to handle situations that occur on the job, who do you seek out?" Another good question to ask job incumbents might be, "When you don't have time to refer to procedures or manuals, who regularly gives you the best and most accurate answers?" (Surprisingly, when you pose this question to a group of incumbents in the same work area or in the same position, you will hear many of the same names.) When your proposed list is complete, get it validated with managers of those particular positions.

3. Arranging for a Participant Mix

It is important that the final group include managers and job incumbents (about four to six). This is a key point: I was asked once to conduct a job analysis for a group of personnel in a manufacturing organization. I specifically asked the department to recommend four to six job incumbents and a couple of managers in the position. I was told that six managers would participate in the session. The organization was not going to send any job incumbents, I was told, because *management* knew what the job incumbents needed to know and do! When I learned this, I sent a note back to the director of the organization and told him that I would not conduct the session unless I had a group of job incumbents to participate, as well. I explained the importance of asking questions to both groups of people simultaneously. The director conceded and subsequently allowed five participants and two managers to participate. As I suspected, there were several discussions about what job incumbents considered their job responsibilities to be, and what management perceived these responsibilities to be. The perceptions were not at all the same. The message I am sending is to stick to your convictions and get the appropriate people in your sessions.

4. Planning Logistics

Once you have a solid list of subject matter experts (SMEs) and a manager for each different position, you can start the logistics planning. Here are a few things that you will need to do prior to the upcoming session:

1. Book a meeting room or space. Arrange to have light snacks and/or coffee, tea, and carbonated beverages for the participants. This tiny gesture makes a huge difference in every participant's impression of the session.

2. Send out invitations (with RSVPs) to the JASR session *two weeks to a month in advance.* Include in the invitation all basic information about the JASR process, date, location, and time. Also stress that the person is being invited because of his or her recognized exemplar performance in the field.

3. Remind participants of the upcoming JASR session—send a brief note or e-mail message about *two weeks prior to the event.*

4. *One week before the session,* verify the room reservation and arrangements for catering services.

5. *One day prior to the session,* make certain that the room is properly set up. Call all the participants and express your appreciation for the time they will share with you. Use this time to answer any last minute questions or to squelch any uneasiness the participant may have at this juncture.

6. *The day of the session,* arrive at least one half-hour early. Complete a brief walk through of the room and make sure all required materials are in place. If coffee and/or other refreshments are to be provided, make sure they are ready for the participants. Create a sign welcoming the participants and identifying the purpose of the session.

5. Gaining Support

One other important activity to undertake prior to the actual session is to do some brief lobbying with key managers and leaders. If possible, showcase some previous sample task lists and related products created for other positions. Answer any questions the manager has and get his or her support. If management backs the process, the right people will probably attend the session.

Now you are ready to conduct the session. You've planned it well. You've got management agreement of the process and you've researched the position you're going to analyze. This up-front work will bring you a huge return on investment in the actual job analysis session that you conduct.

JASR Session Activities

Step 1: Greet the participants and make introductions.

This first step is very important, since it helps set the stage and the tone for the ensuing session. The facilitator and recorder should be there ahead of time to greet the participants. The facilitator and the rest of the group should introduce themselves to set the stage for the session. Use this time to answer any basic questions the participants might have. If you've provided refreshments, offer these to the participants now.

Step 2: Inform participants about the JASR process.

In this step, the facilitator provides a brief overview of the JASR process. The Facilitator also identifies the roles of the Facilitator, Recorder, and Job Incumbents. (Use prefabricated overheads and/or flip charts.) This is a great time to explain to the participants why they have been chosen. Stress the fact the participants have been identified as exemplars by their peers and managers. The job incumbents are the content experts and providers; they will provide most of the information for the job analysis. Inform them that they will be providing information that will be used to help develop or improve training curriculum, organizational planning, behavioral interview guides, etc. This is a good time to show the hierarchical structure of jobs and how they break down into duty areas and tasks. You can use a poster or flip chart for this; prepare them in advance of the session. There is an example of this in Chapter 7.

Step 3: Determine the scope of the job to be analyzed.

It is imperative that the group comes to consensus on the scope of the analysis. If it is too broad, the facilitator will not be able to complete the analysis in a timely fashion. The scope should identify not only what will be analyzed, but also what won't be analyzed. Ask clarifying questions of the group to get this to the most finite level possible. For example, "Do we want to include all sales managers in this job analysis, or only those sales managers who are field-based?" "Do you want to include all of the manufacturing technicians that are at a level 3 or levels 1 through 5?" This critical step will simplify the process from this point forward. When you have identified the job to be analyzed, write the scope at the top of a piece of flip chart paper and put it on the wall.

Step 4: Identify functional areas or duty areas for the job.

Identifying the functional or duty areas (e.g., things like administration, communication, computer skills, problem solving, analytical thinking, etc.) allows for an initial categorization of tasks that will be derived in the next step. This step is used to identify the major groups or "buckets" of similar tasks. It is helpful for the facilitator and the group if they are given some examples of what this might look like for the non-trainers in the group. The author generally uses the "administration" duty areas, since almost all jobs have some type of administrative tasks associated with them. Generally speaking, you should have at least three tasks per duty area. If there are fewer than three task statements in a duty area, it might actually be more appropriate somewhere else.

Use a *round robin* or modified *nominal group technique* method to gather this information. Ask the participants to silently list all of the duty areas they can generate on a piece of scratch paper in front of them. Give the participants a couple of minutes to think about this and write their responses. Now, start with a person in the group and ask the person, "What is the first duty area on your list?" The person responds and two things happen: 1) The facilitator writes the response on the posted flip chart (underneath the job) and 2) each participant looks at his or her list and strikes any similar duty areas. This process continues until the participants have exhausted all of the duty areas. (This helps ensure equitable interaction by all participants.) After the duty areas have been identified, the group can edit the list for conciseness. This is important. As a JASR facilitator, you will want to try to keep the number of duty areas between seven and twelve if possible. You can do this by combining like with like and removing those duty areas that have fewer than three tasks associated with them.

Step 5: Identify tasks within each duty area and note whether they require formal training or non-formal training.

In this step, the facilitator works with the group and helps to identify the tasks associated with the duty area. Most of your participants probably will not have any experience with task statements prior to this activity, so a brief exercise can be conducted to demonstrate how this is done. The facilitator can take any simple duty area, such as phone communication or lawn maintenance (see Table 4-1 below) and have the participants identify tasks associated with them. Another interesting exercise that everyone can relate to is to have the participants silently create a list of those things they did from the time their alarm clocks went off to the time they arrived at the work site. Then ask for the participants to give their task statements one at a time. Someone might say, "Make coffee." Another participant might say, "Take child to school," etc. The bottom line is that with a simple exercise like this, you prove that people with no formal training in writing task statements can create them quite easily. The facilitator might also distribute or show on a flip chart or poster board all the task statement criteria. (There is a sample of this in the Field Book.)

Lawn Maintenance Duty Area
Task Statement
Mow lawn Edge lawn Dispose of lawn clippings Trim hedges Fertilize lawn Water lawn

Table 4-1: Sample Duty Area with Tasks

The facilitator should stress that task statements contain at least an action verb and an object of the verb. Additional qualitative words can be used to make the task more meaningful. For example, if the group uses a certain type of tool or brand name of tool, this could be added to the task. "Use Johnson strainer to filter the lube system," for example. The group now can identify tasks for each of the actual duty areas to be analyzed. After the tasks are identified, have the participants determine if the task statements require formal or non-formal training to learn. *Formal training* is training that is conducted using structured classroom instruction, structured on-the-job training, computer-based training, self-paced training or other training that uses structured methods in the delivery. *Non-formal*

training is any training method, tool, or intervention that is not structured in nature. Examples of this include simple job aids and just-in-time coaching. Mark each task with an "T" or an "NT" to designate this.

Step 6: Print task list and have it signed by the group.

At the end of the session, the recorder prints the task list and has all participants, the facilitator, and the recorder review and sign the task list. The JASR session is now completed. If there is no access to a printer, print the list as soon as possible. You might also distribute a simple evaluation to the participants to gauge their perceptions of the session.

JASR Post-Session Activities

Whew! You've completed a session and things went well. The following are some recommendations of things to do after the session.

1. *Clean the room.* This may seem obvious, but meeting-room space can be very precious in some organizations. If you are a facilitator who expects people to come and clean up after you, the facilities coordinator may not be too anxious to help you out the next time you need meeting space.

2. *Save all flip charts that have recorded information on them.* If you get into a situation where you need to verify something that was said or if you need to clarify a concept, the best way to do it is to refer to the flip charts that were used in the session.

3. *Send out completed task lists to everyone.* In some cases, you may not be able to print the task lists until you get back to your office. If this is the case, make sure that you send a copy of the task list back to the participants and key managers for the position.

4. *Thank the participants and management.* After the session, send out thank you notes, e-mail, or cards to the participants and manager(s). Thank the participants for taking the time away from their jobs and for their willingness to share job information.

5. *Take notes on impressions of the JASR session.* Meet with the recorder after the session and discuss how the session went. Discuss activities that went well. Also discuss those activities that have room for improvement. Keep a log of these discussions for review prior to the next session.

6. *Archive the task list.* For future reference and for your task list portfolio, archive each task list that you complete. Store electronic and hard copies of the validated task lists in a safe location.

Now that you have created a task list, you are probably ready to do something with it. The task list is a foundation for many future deliverables, so the next chapter will discuss these in detail.

Chapter 5
JASR Products and Uses

The primary product of a JASR session is a validated task list. It is the basis for many potential interventions and end products. This chapter explains the ways the validated task list can be used and why the task list is such an integral part of many related products, such as curriculum maps, succession planning documentation, organizational development plans, etc.

Curriculum Development

DEVELOPING TRAINING

The first and most obvious potential use for the validated task list is as the basis for training-curriculum development. The task list contains information about the job, including major duty areas and tasks. It also contains information about the recommended training methodology (i.e., formal or non-formal training). The latter is important because it will help prioritize those tasks for training development. Those tasks that will be taught strictly through formal training should be outlined for training first, since these generally will take the longest time to develop.

The task list helps the training developer get a quick look at the content and skills to be developed. The individual tasks also can be the basis for learning objectives. For instance, if a person has a task under the Communication duty area that is described as, "Make an oral presentation," the task can become the core of the learning objective. All the developer needs to do is add a condition and standard for the performance. A complete learning objective might be constructed like this: "Using Microsoft PowerPoint™, make an oral presentation to persuade an audience." Notice how the task statement "Make an oral presentation" is central to the new learning objective. This learning objective can now be used to create topic modules, and also as the basis for written and performance test items associated with the topic. The training designer or person who has conducted the job analysis can continue this process with the rest of the task statements for the position. When this exercise is completed, you will have a complete list of learning objectives for the position.

These learning objectives can be grouped together in logical order (oftentimes by duty area) to create the major outlines for a lesson plan. Sometimes, one learning objective can be the basis for one module of instruction. In the example that was used earlier ("Using Microsoft PowerPoint™, make an oral presentation to persuade an audience"), you can see that this topic lends itself to a learning intervention of its own. You might develop an entire module around making persuasive presentations with Microsoft PowerPoint™.

Behavioral Interview Guides

One of the next best uses for the validated task list is as a basis for making staffing decisions. This is done in a couple of ways: 1) the task list can be used to create *a behavioral interview guide* for the position, and 2) the task list can be used as the basis for a *job description*. Both of these tools facilitate the staffing process.

The behavioral interview guide is a pivotal tool in conducting perform-ance-based interviews of job candidates. It can easily be built in a template fashion, as follows:

1. Get the most recent revision of the task list.

2. Use a word processor to develop the behavioral interview guide.

3. In the behavioral interview guide, list the job title at the top of the page. For example, the title might be *Accountant Behavioral Interview Guide.*

4. Now, "copy and paste" the task list underneath the title.

5. Create several statements (to be copied and used many times, either as is or in a closely related fashion) such as: "Provide me with an example of a time when you demonstrated . . . (list duty area) skills by (list associated task statement)." For the Accountant position, an example question for the behavioral interview guide might be, "Provide me with an example of a time when you demonstrated *interpersonal skills* by *making an oral presentation.*" Notice that the duty area and a representation of the task statement are in this request. Alternatively, you might request something like, "Describe a time when you demonstrated. . . . (list duty area) skills by (list associated task statement)." Vary the structure a little to create a variety of question types for the behavioral interview guide.

6. Create a statement like this for each duty area and task. The interviewer will now have an entire list of potential interview questions to use. Below are sample questions for an entire *interpersonal skills* duty area.

- Tell me about a time when you demonstrated interpersonal skills by exercising appropriate assertiveness.

- Provide me with an example of a time when you demonstrated interpersonal skills by communicating ideas.

- Describe a time when you demonstrated interpersonal skills by making oral presentations.

- Tell me about a time when you demonstrated interpersonal skills by providing internal customer service.

- Provide me with an example of a time when you demonstrated interpersonal skills by determining people's learning styles/ personality types.

- Describe a time when you demonstrated interpersonal skills by treating people professionally.

- Provide me with an example of a time when you demonstrated interpersonal skills by establishing a good working relationship with the manager.

- Provide me with an example of a time when you demonstrated interpersonal skills by resolving differences with peers or co-workers.

- Describe a time when you demonstrated interpersonal skills by using proper tone/language in written and voice mail communications.

- Provide me with an example of a time when you demonstrated interpersonal skills by communicating with non-financial departments without using finance jargon.

7. Now create spaces in the document to record the interviewee's responses. Finally, add a check box next to the questions. The interviewer can check those questions that he or she asked during the interview.

This is a very powerful, yet basic tool for the interviewer. Using this tool will enable an interviewer to ask task-related questions of the candidate. The manager will need to ask more detailed and probing questions as well as initial questions, but the manager can be sure that the questions will be job-based if the interview questions are created as a result of the JASR process. If the interviewing manager is looking to fill a void in the organization, he or she can pre-select the questions to use based on organizational needs. Because the interview guide had a place to record responses to very specific behavioral questions, several candidates can be compared based on responses to key questions, rather than on the immediate and sometimes subjective perceptions of the interviewer.

Job Descriptions

The next major staffing deliverable associated with the validated task list is the *job description*. Traditionally, job descriptions are vague. The JASR method allows the staffing team to create solid job descriptions very quickly. If your organization is just starting to identify key job positions and analyze them, this method is extremely beneficial for creating job descriptions. Each position is chunked nicely by duty area and groups of tasks, so the job description author can go as light or as high-level or as detailed as desired. A job description could list the duty areas as general responsibilities and then include some (or all) of the tasks to specify the job at a detailed level.

Job Incumbent Self-Assessment

Job incumbents can evaluate themselves with the task list. The incumbent can review the task list periodically to determine which tasks he or she cannot perform in order to help identify developmental needs. Sometimes managers will identify levels of performance for each task on the task list.

They create behavioral indicators and scales that are associated with various performance levels. (See the Loan Processor University Federal Credit Union Self-Assessment in the Field Book, as an example.)

Performance Management

In a similar vein, managers can use the task list to facilitate the performance of personnel they manage. Each individual contributor working in a position can be rated in areas of the task list that are part of their job. This is an important thing to remember. Generally speaking, not every person in a certain position will be 100% proficient at all the tasks on a task list. It is imperative that the manager knows those tasks on which the job incumbent will be rated. In this way, specific feedback can be given periodically and during the review cycle.

Organizational Planning

Another great use for the task list is in organizational planning. It is possible to create a matrix for an entire organization of people with the same position against a task list. Each individual is listed, as well as each task. Checks or Xs can be used to identify whether or not a person is qualified at a task. Alternatively, the manager can place a "D" in a slot for developmental, or "P" for proficient. A sample set of tasks is matrixed in Table 5-1.

Task Statement	Avery	Cruz	Johnson	Kovach	Miller	Roberts	Trevino	Willis
Exercise appropriate assertiveness.	X	X		X		X		X
Communicate ideas.		X		X				
Make oral presentations.			X					
Provide internal customer service.		X			X			X
Determine people's learning styles/personality types.	X	X		X				
Treat people professionally.	X		X		X	X		X
Establish a good working relationship with the manager.		X			X		X	
Resolve differences with peers or co-workers.	X	X						
Use proper tone/language in all written or voice mail communications.		X	X	X				
Communicate with non-financial departments without using finance jargon.					X	X		X

Table 5-1

One can start to draw some conclusions about this organization relatively quickly. The first thing that we can see is that Cruz is the most qualified individual on the team. She is qualified in seven out of ten tasks that have been identified as important. The second bit of information you can see quickly is that Trevino is the least qualified individual on the team. This fits in this case, since he is the newest member of the team. Several other conclusions can be drawn from the matrix. People on the team are the least proficient at the "Make oral presentations" task. Two other tasks are weak: "Communicate ideas," and "Resolve differences with peers or co-workers." These might be areas that the manager can focus training and coaching sessions on.

The matrix also helps the manager make some good decisions about who to hire when the next spot is open. Since the team is so weak in communication and resolving differences, it would be beneficial to ask behavioral interview questions related to those tasks. For example, "Tell me about a time when you demonstrated interpersonal skills by resolving differences you had with a peer." You can see how powerful an organizational matrix like this can be.

Competency Development

There is another powerful deliverable that can be derived from the validated task list: competencies. "Competencies are underlying characteristics of people and indicate ways of behaving or thinking, generalizing across situations, and enduring for a reasonably long period of time." (Spencer, p. 9) In order for an individual to perform jobs at an appropriate level, he or she must possess the requisite competencies for the position. One of the best ways to determine the requisite competencies is through an analysis of the validated task list. A person can analyze a task list for commonalties and clusters that fit into a major competency group. If you are not sure about what some competency groups are, you can use a book like *Spencer's Competence at Work* that contains a robust competency dictionary to refer to. Just assess the duty areas and tasks that are present against the competency dictionary that is in the text (or similar books). If you don't have a competency dictionary to refer to, you can create competencies for a position based on logical groupings of tasks. Sometimes the duty areas can give you clues. Examples that come to mind are *Interpersonal Understanding* (Remember the interpersonal skills duty area used earlier?), *Analytical Thinking, Relationship Building,* etc. Groups of competencies for a position are called *competency models*. The competency model gives the end-user a quick snapshot of the knowledge, skills, and abilities required for success on the job.

The earlier discussion has provided you with some examples and ways that the task list can be used. There are others that you may generate as well. The key to remember is that the by-products you create from the validated task list are extremely valuable because they are based on actual job needs, and not on the whims of a training or human resource organization. You can use the task list as the basis for curriculum development, behavioral interview guides, job descriptions, performance management, organizational planning, and competency development.

In the next chapter, you will learn some of the finer points to remember as a facilitator. Excellent facilitation skills are important for successful implementation of this job analysis method.

Chapter 6
Facilitation Tips for the JASR Method

The facilitator for the JASR Method is a very important person. Without competent facilitation and content expertise, there will be no task list produced. Job incumbents must rely on the facilitator to coach them through this process, since most people will not have seen this method previously. There is also a high likelihood (except in the case of training and human resource functions) that the *job analysis* concept will be a very foreign notion for most participants. This section will describe some traits, tips, and techniques the JASR Facilitator can use to ensure that the job analysis session is a success.

Skills and Traits of a Good Facilitator

There are many skills and traits an artful facilitator should possess. These are identified below.

Skills

Influence—Facilitators must use influence skills to help guide the job incumbents in the job analysis session. This is truly an important skill because most of the participants will never have used or participated in any job study activities.

Conceptual Thinking—Facilitators must recognize emerging patterns in the job analysis. This includes taking large chunks of information and breaking them down into component parts. The facilitator invariably will be synthesizing information to try to make sense of it.

Interpersonal Skills—The facilitator who is overly assertive or domineering will fail. Participants will respond much more openly to those facilitators who listen and communicate well with them. The facilitator must be able to navigate the attitudes and feelings their participants have during the session. The facilitator must be tactful and responsive to his or her participants. If the participant ever says (either verbally or nonverbally) "I don't want to be here," neither will his or her participants.

Empathy—The skilled facilitator is aware of the feelings of the audience that he or she is working with in the job analysis process. Because the facilitator has done adequate research prior to the actual JASR session, he or she is aware of the environmental, organizational, political, and strategic issues that participants experience on a daily basis. Demonstrating empathy with the group accelerates the credibility of the facilitator and catalyzes in-depth and candid discussions of the job being analyzed.

Humor—Even though job analysis is a serious activity, the adroit facilitator uses appropriate humor to establish rapport with the participant job incumbents and to diffuse potentially heated discussions. Be careful not to be hurtful with any humor or jokes that you use. Be cautious about making comments that reflect personal agendas or bias. It is inappropriate to defame or ridicule any individuals or groups of people.

Technical Knowledge—As a facilitator for JASR, you must have technical knowledge about facilitation techniques and job analysis processes. However, before you conduct any sessions, it is wise to research the position(s) you are going to analyze to gather key technical information about the position. See Chapter 4 for more information on this topic.

Conflict Resolution Skills—Because of the nature of these sessions, discussions can sometimes get rather heated. Managers and individual contributors often disagree on duty areas, tasks, or responsibilities. Some individuals take these "differences of opinion" personally and will gladly share these feelings with any of the other participants in the group. The facilitator's job is to arbitrate these types of discussions. Allow both sides to get their points across and get consensus with the group. You can moderate these friction points and help the group come to agreement at an appropriate middle ground. Remember that everybody is important in these discussions, and all input is valuable. Additionally, remember that although arguments can seem draining, they can also bolster creativity in a group.

Problem Solving (Analytical Thinking)—Job analysis involves a myriad of problems and puzzling situations that you as the facilitator must help solve. You've got to be decisive and flexible. The ability to "think on your feet" is crucial to your success. The participants will look to you for guidance and to remove obstacles when the job analysis gets into areas of uncertainty. I recommend that you call on the vast body of knowledge possessed by the participants when problems arise.

Feedback Skills—As the facilitator, you will often have to give succinct and constructive feedback to the participants (and possibly the recorder as well). Give appropriate feedback as soon as it is appropriate. Guide participants' responses early if they are not providing the appropriate answers to questions you pose. For example, if participants are using action verbs that are weak (such as "understand" or "know") in their tasks, then immediately inform the respondents of this and provide other examples as well. (A sample verb list for task statements is included in the Field Book.)

Decision-making—As mentioned before, the JASR method will be a new and unexplored method for most people. There will be times when the group will enter into discussions about duty areas or tasks or some other area of the analysis that can potentially stall the analysis. One of your jobs as the facilitator is to help keep the participants on track and help the group make appropriate decisions. Compare and contrast information you get from the session and make recommendations about the job analysis when questions arise. One interesting point to make about this method is that because job analysis can be conducted so quickly, if the job analysis is not 100% accurate initially, subsequent analyses can be conducted to validate the list that has been created. Jobs change quickly enough that task lists will always be evolving slightly.

Time management—To complete the job analysis in three hours or less, the adroit facilitator will manage time for the process with precision. It is easy for side discussions, non-session related activities, and other distractions to whittle away at the time that you have to conduct the job analysis session. Envision the session prior to actually conducting it. Identify major blocks of time and how the time will be spent to get the information needed. Don't let one duty area or set of tasks in the analysis consume all of your time. Budget time to get all of the information you can from the participants. The needs of the company may get in the way of your speaking with these individuals after this session, so don't waste the opportunity.

Traits

Credibility—This is an important trait for the facilitator. You've got to have credibility and be perceived as credible with the group you are working with to maximize participation. Ways that you can become credible with the group include: starting the session at the appointed time, researching the position you are analyzing, focusing on process, responding truthfully and accurately to questions, and most importantly, keeping all promises. If you tell a participant, "I'll get back to you on that," then you will increase your personal credibility by doing so.

Adaptive and Flexible—Job analyses, like rivers, flow at different rates and intensities. No two groups of people will think or act the exact same way. It is imperative that you be able to respond to the many ways participants will respond to this method. As the group leader for the session, you've got to be able to exhibit flexibility during the job analysis.

Persevering—Stick with the analysis! In some groups and with some jobs, the JASR method can seem like it doesn't make sense or that the outcomes will be worthless. If the facilitator displays this type of an attitude, the participants will quickly disengage from the session.

Agenda-free—It would be easy for the facilitator to force his or her agenda on the job analysis session. This is not desirable, however, because it weakens your credibility. Leave your personal agendas out of the session. Remember that this job analysis is for the job incumbents and their respective departments. Your responsibility is to get the most objective look at the job to be analyzed. That's hard to do when you go into a session with your personal agendas.

We've discussed some of the skills and traits necessary for JASR facilitators. In the next section, some specific facilitation techniques will be identified and explained.

Nominal Group Technique

The *Nominal Group Technique* (NGT) method is a key tool used in the JASR process. It is a "... structured small-group process for generating ideas." (Higgins, p. 150) The NGT method is used in the focus group to help answer the main questions of the job analysis, such as, "What are the duty areas for the job to be analyzed?" and subsequently, "What are the tasks for each duty area?" This method helps keep people who monopolize discussions in check. The nature of the NGT is round-robin, so when a question is asked, each person gets to respond—but it is done in order.

ROUND ROBIN

The major steps of the Nominal Group Technique are as follows:

1. The facilitator asks a question of the group.

2. Each participant silently generates responses on a piece of paper.

3. The facilitator asks each participant in turn to answer the question. As a participant states his or her answer, the other participants strike similar answers from their lists.

4. The facilitator captures the responses on a flip chart at the front of the room.

5. When all of the participants have exhausted the responses on the list, review the list to make sure that it is as succinct and meaningful as possible. This may mean that the facilitator goes back and assimilates responses and creates more meaningful groupings.

6. The facilitator makes sure that everyone agrees with the changes made to the final list.

Now, the facilitator is ready to move to the next question or step in the process.

Gaining Consensus

An important objective the facilitator has to meet in every session is to gain consensus. If the group members answer questions and work together as a group but never feel like they can agree with the rest of the group, the JASR process will not be successful. The facilitator must guide this process and use questioning and feedback techniques to ensure that all of the participants feel like they can "live with" the outcome. It is important to note that absolute consensus with a group of six to eight people may never occur (it can be difficult for two people to agree on some things). However, the facilitator needs to ascertain as accurately as possible the consensus level of the group. When the facilitator is relatively certain that consensus exists in the group, the facilitator can lead the group in the next activity.

In this chapter, you learned about the traits, skills, and knowledge necessary for excellent facilitation during the JASR process. You've also learned about some specific techniques (*nominal group technique* and *gaining consensus*). In the next chapter we will discuss ways that job analysis will be conducted in the future, and also provide a summary of the key points from the book.

Chapter 7
Summary and a Peek into the Future

In the previous chapters of this book, you've discovered some of the background information you will need to conduct an actual JASR session. You've read about the nightmarish experiences of others, been given an overview of the JASR process, and reviewed a few of the methods used to conduct job analysis. You've also identified the steps in the JASR process, been briefed on the major products of JASR, and learned about the competencies required if one is to be an artful facilitator. The central message I hope you have received and understood is that this method is 1) quick, 2) easy to conduct, 3) and valid. You can use Job Analysis at the Speed of Reality to gather information that will form the foundation for many subsequent products.

The first couple of times that you conduct JASR sessions may feel uncomfortable. You might get into a couple of tough situations during the analysis that require you to problem-solve on your feet. That's okay! Go with it. Each time you do this, you'll get a little smoother and you'll become more comfortable with the process.

You will usually conduct JASR sessions in a classroom or meeting room. However, growing use of collaborative tools, teleconferencing, and other computer-based link-ups will create opportunities for asynchronous and synchronous job analysis opportunities. They enable the facilitator to conduct sessions in one remote location, hooked up to participants hundreds or thousands of miles away. Let's set up a scenario and explore how you can do this.

There are many collaborative learning and application tools on the market today. Products such as Reachout™, Microsoft NetMeeting™, and Databeam's Learning Server™ allow real-time collaboration and application-sharing over networks and the Internet. A facilitator can set up a teleconference with six field sales representatives in six different locations, while simultaneously displaying appropriate slides and posing questions. Every person in each of the remote locations can hear the facilitator asking questions (just like in a face-to-face meeting) and view the same overheads or slides that a facilitator might use in a classroom. After such a session, the field sales representatives can return to work, handling their respective accounts without incurring costs associated with lost sales time (after the session, the reps can immediately service their accounts) or travel costs to attend sessions at a central location (each of the participants remain at their home office). Another intangible benefit is that the remote personnel see this as a value-added service that the HR or Organizational Development (OD) function has provided (there is minimal disruption to the business).

If you don't have access to some of the aforementioned software applications, most of the interviews can be handled during regular teleconferences with the job analysis participants. Here's how you can do it:

1. Prior to the JASR session, send out an informational packet with an overview and a summary of what you expect from the participants. (You might remind them to bring this to the session.)

2. Set a date and time for the analysis and make arrangements for everyone to participate at that time.

3. Now conduct the session using the teleconference technology like you normally would.

4. Thank all the participants when it is over, and send each of them a completed task list.

You can also use e-mail to conduct these sessions in an asynchronous fashion. However, this method will take much longer than three hours and require more work on the facilitator's part. The facilitator should send out (via e-mail) an informational note to the participants about what JASR is and what each of them will be expected to contribute. A couple of days later, the facilitator can send out the first e-mail to the participants, asking the question, "What is the scope of the job we are going to analyze?" Once the responses are returned, the facilitator synthesizes the information and e-mails it out with the next question: "What are the duty areas of your job?" The facilitator compiles the responses, creates the composite list and sends it back to the participants, along with the question, "What are the task statements for each of the duty areas for this job?" When the responses are gathered from this last question, the facilitator can create the valid task list, which is then mailed to all of the participants. This method tends to be relatively time consuming, and will be harder to complete because of the synthesis that must be done for each question. The synergy of a focus group is also lost with this method. "Threaded" discussions might be used allow the participants to cumulatively build on each other's responses.

"NICE TO MEET YOU!"

There is no limit to the way technology can be applied to leverage processes—the only limitations are on what you can or cannot imagine. When you start to use the JASR method, think of other ways you can implement it using technology to streamline and expedite the process.

The next section is the Field Book, which contains all of the facilitator guides, overheads, etc., that you will need to facilitate JASR sessions on your own. Now that you've got a good theoretical understanding of JASR and the right tools, you're ready to facilitate a few job analysis sessions.

The JASR Field Book

How Do I Use the JASR Field Book?

Now that you know the theory behind the Job Analysis at the Speed of Reality method, you will find this Field Book helpful in conducting job analysis sessions for yourself and others.

The JASR Field Book includes the following:

- the facilitator guide

- overhead projector slides

- a sample behavioral interview guide

- a list of action verbs

- templates

- sample task lists

- a materials checklist

- a glossary and list of acronyms

- job analysis Internet resources

- a bibliography.

Each of the tools and templates included in the Field Book are designed to help you analyze and assess job tasks and responsibilities easily.

Facilitator Guide—Job Analysis at the Speed of Reality (JASR)

Overview

Use this Facilitator Guide to assist you with the facilitation of the job analysis session.

**Step 1
Greet participants and make introductions**

Be at the appointed job analysis location early enough to greet participants as they arrive. Tell the participants your name and find out who they are. You can also use this time to start answering questions. Be friendly and courteous. If you have refreshments for the participants, offer them.

Participant Introductions

When all of the participants have arrived, briefly introduce yourself to the group and ask each participant to introduce himself or herself. Each participant should state his or her name, job title, department, and role in the job analysis session.

Participant appreciation and JASR time-estimate

The facilitator should explain that the process is going to take between two and three hours. Thank participants for their willingness to share their experiences with you and the rest of the group.

**Step 2
Inform participants about the JASR session**

Provide an overview of the JASR process and major steps:

The Six-Step JASR Process

Note: The overview can be put on a flip chart so that it can be referred to during the session.

1. *Greet the participants and conduct introductions.*
2. *Inform participants about the JASR process.*
3. *Determine the scope of the job to be analyzed.*
4. *Identify functional areas or duty areas for the job.*
5. *Identify tasks within each duty area and whether they require formal training or non-formal training.*
6. *Print the task list and have it signed by the group.*

Discuss key roles for the JASR process including:

- Facilitator (Process Role)
- Recorder (Process Role)
- Participant or Job Incumbent (Content Role)

Stress the importance of each person's participation and explain that together they possess all the content knowledge that is necessary for completion of the job analysis.

(continued)

Facilitator Guide—Job Analysis at the Speed of Reality (JASR)
(continued)

Step 3
Determine the scope of the job to be analyzed

It is imperative that the "right" job is analyzed. The facilitator must make certain that the job to be analyzed is not too narrow or too broad in scope.

Ask questions and survey the group and managers present to get the most appropriate level for the content.

Write the job title on a piece of flip chart paper and post the page on the wall for all to see.

Step 4
Identify functional areas or duty areas for the job

a. Use a round-robin technique to uncover the duty areas for the job that is being scoped. *Ask: "What major groupings of tasks do you do?"* It is a good idea to provide an example for people to relate to. For example, ask people to think of all of the "administrative" tasks they do as a part of their jobs. Most people have to attend meetings, respond to voice mail, complete expense reports, etc. Use this example to help clarify what a duty or functional area is.

b. Have each participant write his or her duty areas on the scratch paper provided. Allow three to five minutes for participants to complete this step. While the participants are doing this, write "Duty Areas" on a piece of flip chart paper in the front of the room. When time has elapsed, *ask: "What's your first duty area?"* Capture the participant's response on the flip chart. Each of the other participants should strike the same or similar responses from their lists. Continue this activity in round-robin fashion until there are no other duty areas identified.

c. Examine the finished list. How long is it? If there are 8—13 duty or functional areas, then an appropriate number of duty areas have been identified. If there are many more than that (which happens often), work with the group to consolidate the list. Reorganize and rename similar duty areas to whittle the list down to an appropriate size. Make sure that tasks are not identified instead of duty areas; duty areas should have at least three distinct tasks associated with them.

d. When the group has come to consensus about the final duty areas, post the list on the wall. The facilitator may have to rewrite the lists because they cannot be easily read from a distance.

Make sure that the "recorder" has noted the duty areas on the task list template.

(continued)

Facilitator Guide—Job Analysis at the Speed of Reality (JASR)
(continued)

Step 5
Identify tasks within each duty area and whether each requires formal training or non-formal training

Note the number of duty areas that have to be analyzed. Budget time to determine tasks accordingly. For example, if there are 10 duty areas to identify tasks and 90 minutes left, spend only about 8 minutes per duty area.

a. Inform the group that the next step is to identify task statements from the duty areas that were identified in the previous step. A round-robin technique will be used as in the previous steps.

b. If participants are not familiar with task statements, give them a brief example. Ask the participants: "What have you done from the time you woke up until you arrived at work?" Tell them that there needs to be at least an action verb and an object of the verb to have an actual task statement. Have each person create two task statements based on the aforementioned criteria. Direct the participants to read their task statements (in a round-robin fashion). Briefly critique the examples provided as necessary. Remind the participants about how easy it was to do this.

c. Now, repeat the process using the actual duty areas that were identified in the previous step. Choose a duty area from the list and write it at the top of a piece of flip chart paper in large letters with a water-based marker.

d. Direct the participants to write a list of task statements for the duty area that has been chosen on the scratch paper provided. Allow three to five minutes for this part of the exercise. When time has elapsed, ask a participant to share the first task statement on the list. Write the task statement on the flip chart; the other participants should cross off similar task statements from their lists. Continue this until the participants have offered all of the task statements. As necessary, provide guidance to the participants on task statements. (They need to at least contain a solid action verb and an object for the verb.) Refer to the action verb list in the field book, if necessary. In fact, it's a good idea to have a copy of the list duplicated for each participant to refer to during this portion of the job analysis.

e. Once the task statements are recorded for the duty area, go back and ask the participants, "What kind of training do you need to learn each task?" Read the first task statement and determine whether or not the participants need formal (T) or non-formal (NT) training to learn the task. Formal training includes classroom or computer-based training, structured on-the-job training, structured web training, etc. Non-formal training includes the use of job aids, informal mentoring, and on-the-job experience. It is possible that some task statements may get rated as both formal and non-formal or (T/NT). Post the completed flip chart on one of the side walls.

(continued)

Facilitator Guide—Job Analysis at the Speed of Reality (JASR)
(concluded)

Step 5 *(continued)*

 f. Repeat steps 5c, 5d, and 5e above until all task statements have been identified and rated for training type for all duty areas.

Make certain that the recorder has captured all of the information in the template.

Step 6
Print task list and have
it signed by the group

 a. Send the participants on a brief break (5 minutes or so).
 b. Save the completed task to a floppy disk.
 c. Locate a printer.
 d. Print the completed task list.
 e. When the participants return from the break, have them sign and date the task list.
 f. If possible, make copies of the completed task list for each of the participants.

Summarize

Thank the participants for their time and effort. Let the participants know that they can call you after the job analysis session is completed if they need to. Release the participants back to their work.

Breakdown of a Job

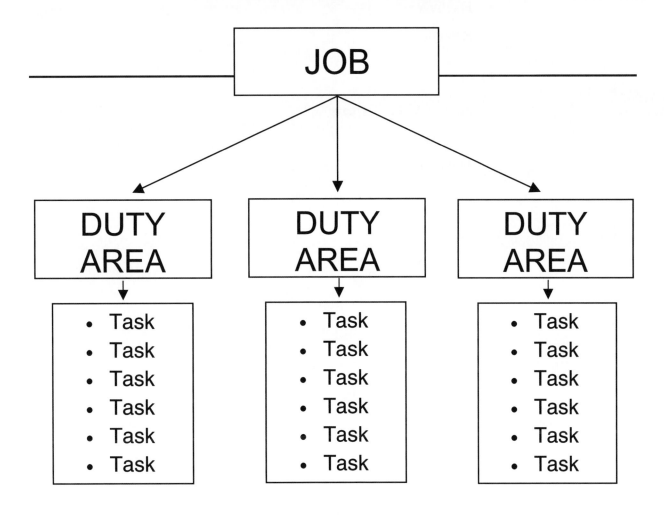

Roles

Process

- Facilitator
- Recorder

Content

- Subject Matter Experts
- Supervisor
- Manager

JASR* Steps

1. Greet the participants and make introductions.

2. Inform participants about the JASR process.

3. Determine the scope of the job to be analyzed.

4. Identify functional areas or duty areas for the job.

5. Identify tasks within each duty area and whether they require formal training or non-formal training.

6. Print the task list and have it signed by the group.

*Job Analysis at the Speed of Reality

Task Statement Criteria

- Contains at least an action verb and an object of the verb

- Can stand alone

- Uses job-related terminology

- Uses only one concrete action verb per statement

- Should be as succinct as possible (try to keep task statements to eight words or less)

- Reflects observable activities

- Completion of task should result in product, service, decision, or other recognizable deliverable

Sample Behavioral Interview Guides

Accountant Behavioral-Interview Guide

Use the following guide to gather information about potential candidates for an Accountant position.

Administrative	
Administrative Tasks	**Interviewer Comments**
Provide an example of a time when you demonstrated strong *administrative skills* by finalizing a spreadsheet.	
Provide an example of a time when you demonstrated strong *administrative skills* by developing a checklist.	
Provide an example of a time when you demonstrated strong *administrative skills* by making copies.	
Provide an example of a time when you demonstrated strong *administrative skills* by composing meeting notes and agendas.	
Provide an example of a time when you demonstrated strong *administrative skills* by planning month-end (close) duties.	
Provide an example of a time when you demonstrated strong *administrative skills* by improving processes.	
Provide an example of a time when you demonstrated strong *administrative skills* by filing paper work.	
Provide an example of a time when you demonstrated strong *administrative skills* by routing paperwork.	

(continued)

Administrative Tasks	Interviewer Comments
Provide an example of a time when you demonstrated strong *administrative skills* by composing policy/process documentation.	
Provide an example of a time when you demonstrated strong *administrative skills* by attending meetings.	
Provide an example of a time when you demonstrated strong *administrative skills* by scheduling meetings.	
Provide an example of a time when you demonstrated strong *administrative skills* by finding supporting documentation (pulling invoices).	
Provide an example of a time when you demonstrated strong *administrative skills* by responding to written mail.	
Financial Analysis	
Financial Analysis	**Interviewer Comments**
Provide an example of a time when you demonstrated strong *financial analysis skills* by reviewing expense information.	
Provide an example of a time when you demonstrated strong *financial analysis skills* by identifying variances prior to the current period.	
Provide an example of a time when you demonstrated strong *financial analysis skills* by comparing actuals to forecasts.	
Provide an example of a time when you demonstrated strong *financial analysis skills* by researching reconciliations.	

(continued)

Financial Analysis	Interviewer Comments
Provide an example of a time when you demonstrated strong *financial analysis skills* by calculating ratios to determine cause and effect (e.g. D80).	
Provide an example of a time when you demonstrated strong *financial analysis skills* by reporting root cause analysis of variance.	
Provide an example of a time when you demonstrated strong *financial analysis skills* by researching variances	
Provide an example of a time when you demonstrated strong *financial analysis skills* by formulating conclusions.	
Provide an example of a time when you demonstrated strong *financial analysis skills* by taking corrective actions.	
Provide an example of a time when you demonstrated strong *financial analysis skills* by using financial software to gather data.	
Provide an example of a time when you demonstrated strong *financial analysis skills* by generating reports.	
Provide an example of a time when you demonstrated strong *financial analysis skills* by reviewing financial analysis reports.	
Provide an example of a time when you demonstrated strong *financial analysis skills* by evaluating metrics.	

(continued)

Core Fundamentals	
Core Fundamentals	**Interviewer Comments**
Provide an example of a time when you demonstrated strong *financial analysis skills* by providing information to the financial analysts for forecasting.	
Provide an example of a time when you demonstrated strong knowledge of *core fundamentals* by attending new hire orientation.	
Provide an example of a time when you demonstrated strong knowledge of *core fundamentals* by describing the Dell Finance ethics policy.	
Provide an example of a time when you demonstrated strong knowledge of *core fundamentals* by stating how the Dell Finance organization works.	
Provide an example of a time when you demonstrated strong knowledge of *core fundamentals* by describing Dell's product lines (LOB).	
Provide an example of a time when you demonstrated strong knowledge of *core fundamentals* by using Dell terminology.	
Provide an example of a time when you demonstrated strong knowledge of *core fundamentals* by stating the meaning of core accounting terms (e.g., balance sheet, income statement, general ledger, account reconciliation).	
Provide an example of a time when you demonstrated strong knowledge of *core fundamentals* by describing the Dell close process.	

(continued)

Core Fundamentals	Interviewer Comments
Provide an example of a time when you demonstrated strong knowledge of *core fundamentals* by describing Dell Financial software systems and inter-relationships.	
Provide an example of a time when you demonstrated strong knowledge of *core fundamentals* by describing the Dell and Dell Finance organizations.	

Process Management

Process Management	Interviewer Comments
Provide an example of a time when you demonstrated strong *process management skills* by identifying finance processes.	
Provide an example of a time when you demonstrated strong *process management skills* by stating the internal controls for finance.	
Provide an example of a time when you demonstrated strong *process management skills* by using internal controls.	
Provide an example of a time when you demonstrated strong *process management skills* by creating a data flow chart by organization (P&L and income statements by department).	
Provide an example of a time when you demonstrated strong *process management skills* by making certain that all close processes are completed as scheduled.	

(continued)

Process Management	Interviewer Comments
Provide an example of a time when you demonstrated strong *process management skills* by describing the balance sheet review process (including players/participants).	

Interpersonal Skills	

Interpersonal Skills	Interviewer Comments
Provide an example of a time when you demonstrated strong *interpersonal skills* by exercising appropriate assertiveness.	
Provide an example of a time when you demonstrated strong *interpersonal skills* by communicating ideas.	
Provide an example of a time when you demonstrated strong *interpersonal skills* by making oral presentations.	
Provide an example of a time when you demonstrated strong *interpersonal skills* by providing internal customer service.	
Provide an example of a time when you demonstrated strong *interpersonal skills* by determining people's learning styles/ personality types.	
Provide an example of a time when you demonstrated strong *interpersonal skills* by treating people professionally.	
Provide an example of a time when you demonstrated strong *interpersonal skills* by establishing a good working relationship with a manager.	

(continued)

Interpersonal Skills	Interviewer Comments
Provide an example of a time when you demonstrated strong *interpersonal skills* by resolving differences with peers or a co-worker.	
Provide an example of a time when you demonstrated strong *interpersonal skills* by using proper tone/language in written mail or voice mail communications.	
Provide an example of a time when you demonstrated strong *interpersonal skills* by communicating with non-financial departments without using finance jargon.	
Problem Solving/Root Cause	
Problem Solving/Root Cause	**Interviewer Comments**
Provide an example of a time when you demonstrated strong *problem-solving skills* by establishing a system that identifies problems on a recurring basis.	
Provide an example of a time when you demonstrated strong *problem-solving skills* by defining the problem.	
Provide an example of a time when you demonstrated strong *problem-solving skills* by using software to research a cause.	
Provide an example of a time when you demonstrated strong *problem-solving skills* by identifying the financial impact of a problem.	
Provide an example of a time when you demonstrated strong *problem-solving skills* by determining who the problem affects.	

(continued)

Problem Solving/Root Cause	Interviewer Comments
Provide an example of a time when you demonstrated strong *problem-solving skills* by conducting a meeting with affected people.	
Provide an example of a time when you demonstrated strong *problem-solving skills* by developing an action plan.	
Provide an example of a time when you demonstrated strong *problem-solving skills* by identifying necessary steps.	
Provide an example of a time when you demonstrated strong *problem-solving skills* by determining resolutions.	
Provide an example of a time when you demonstrated strong *problem-solving skills* by implementing an action plan/ resolution.	
Provide an example of a time when you demonstrated strong *problem-solving skills* by following up on a resolution.	
Project Management	
Project Management	**Interviewer Comments**
Provide an example of a time when you demonstrated strong *project management skills* by attending project meetings.	
Provide an example of a time when you demonstrated strong *project management skills* by determining action items/issues.	
Provide an example of a time when you demonstrated strong *project management skills* by completing action items (to an appropriate level).	

(continued)

Project Management	Interviewer Comments
Provide an example of a time when you demonstrated strong *project management skills* by identifying a project objective.	
Provide an example of a time when you demonstrated strong *project management skills* by identifying the client/sponsor.	
Provide an example of a time when you demonstrated strong *project management skills* by ensuring implementation.	
Provide an example of a time when you demonstrated strong *project management skills* by acting as a finance representative for various projects.	
Reconciliation Issue Analysis	
Reconciliation Issue Analysis	**Interviewer Comments**
Provide an example of a time when you demonstrated strong *reconciliation issue analysis skills* by inputting data to the DOMS and (ROSS) general ledger.	
Provide an example of a time when you demonstrated strong *reconciliation issue analysis skills* by generating a reconciliation schedule.	
Provide an example of a time when you demonstrated strong *reconciliation issue analysis skills* by reconciling accounts manually.	
Provide an example of a time when you demonstrated strong *reconciliation issue analysis skills* by conducting aging reports (flags for how long in system).	

(continued)

Reconciliation Issue Analysis	Interviewer Comments
Provide an example of a time when you demonstrated strong *reconciliation issue analysis skills* by identifying reconciling items.	
Provide an example of a time when you demonstrated strong *reconciliation issue analysis skills* by determining materiality for reconciling items.	
Provide an example of a time when you demonstrated strong *reconciliation issue analysis skills* by researching data for reconciliations.	
Provide an example of a time when you demonstrated strong *reconciliation issue analysis skills* by using Hyperion/ROSS.	
Provide an example of a time when you demonstrated strong *reconciliation issue analysis skills* by determining corrective action.	
Provide an example of a time when you demonstrated strong *reconciliation issue analysis skills* by taking corrective action.	

Sample Action Verb List

This is a list of action verbs you might find useful when formulating tasks. These are explicit action verbs that can be used to help formulate clear task statements.

accomplish	conduct	explain	monitor	replenish
achieve	confront	express	motivate	report
add	consolidate	facilitate	navigate	represent
adjust	construct	forecast	negotiate	research
administer	control	fulfill	observe	resolve
adopt	coordinate	generate	operate	respond
advise	correspond	guide	organize	revamp
advocate	counsel	hire	originate	review
aid	create	identify	participate	revise
allocate	critique	implement	perform	rewrite
analyze	decide	induce	persuade	schedule
apply	delegate	influence	plan	secure
appraise	demonstrate	inform	predict	select
approve	describe	initiate	prepare	sell
arbitrate	design	illustrate	present	serve
arrange	determine	imagine	print	simplify
assemble	develop	inspect	prioritize	sketch
assess	diagnose	inspire	process	solve
assign	differentiate	install	produce	speak
assist	dispatch	instruct	program	streamline
attain	dispense	integrate	project	strengthen
audit	display	interpret	promote	succeed
budget	dissect	interview	proofread	summarize
calibrate	distribute	invent	propose	supervise
care (for)	document	investigate	provide	synthesize
change	draft	involve	publish	systematize
check	draw	judge	question	teach
clarify	earn	launch	raise	theorize
classify	educate	lead	recommend	train
coach	edit	lecture	reconcile	transact
code	effect	lobby	record	transfer
collate	encourage	locate	recruit	translate
collect	enlist	maintain	refer	treat
communicate	establish	manage	reduce	update
compete	estimate	map	regulate	upgrade
compile	evaluate	measure	rehabilitate	verify
complete	examine	mediate	reorganize	write
compose	exhibit	mentor	repair	
compute	expedite	model	replace	

Templates

This section contains several templates that you can use to conduct the JASR session.

The first template is used to gather job analysis data to create the valid task list.

JASR Template for Task List

Job to be Analyzed:
Date:
Location:
Facilitator:
Recorder:

Duty Area 1:		
Task Number	**Task Statement**	**Formal (T) or Non-Formal Training (NT)**

Duty Area 2:		
Task Number	**Task Statement**	**Formal (T) or Non-Formal Training (NT)**

\multicolumn{3}{c}{Duty Area 3:}		

Task Number	Task Statement	Formal (T) or Non-Formal Training (NT)

\multicolumn{3}{c}{Duty Area 4:}		

Task Number	Task Statement	Formal (T) or Non-Formal Training (NT)

Duty Area 5:		
Task Number	Task Statement	Formal (T) or Non-Formal Training (NT)

Duty Area 6:		
Task Number	Task Statement	Formal (T) or Non-Formal Training (NT)

Duty Area 7:		
Task Number	**Task Statement**	**Formal (T) or Non-Formal Training (NT)**

Duty Area 8:		
Task Number	**Task Statement**	**Formal (T) or Non-Formal Training (NT)**

	Duty Area 9:		
Task Number	**Task Statement**	**Formal (T) or Non-Formal Training (NT)**

	Duty Area 10:		
Task Number	**Task Statement**	**Formal (T) or Non-Formal Training (NT)**

Duty Area 11:		
Task Number	**Task Statement**	**Formal (T) or Non-Formal Training (NT)**

Signature Section:

JASR Role	**Job Title**	**Signature**	**Date**
Facilitator			
Recorder			
Participant			
Participant			
Participant			
Participant			
Participant			
Participant			
Participant			
Participant			

Materials Checklist and Setup

☐ One box of water-based flip chart markers

☐ Two pads of flip chart paper (preferably 3M™)

☐ Scratch paper

☐ Pencils and/or pens for participants to use

☐ Portable computer

☐ Blank disk

☐ Printer or access to a printer

☐ Name tents for participants

☐ Two flip chart stands

☐ Any necessary pre-fabricated flip charts (e.g., in case you want to show the hierarchical breakdown of jobs, duty areas, and tasks)

Sample Task Lists

This is a sample task list that was created for Dell Accountants. It includes an outline of the major steps of the process, as well as the completed task list.

Accountant—JASR SESSION

Job to be Analyzed: Accountant (Exempt)
Date:
Location: Round Rock 2
Facilitator: Darin Hartley
Recorder: Vickie Floyd

Duty Area 1: Administrative		
Task Number	**Task Statement**	**Formal (T) or Non-Formal Training (NT)**
1.	Finalize spreadsheet	(NT/T)
2.	Develop checklist	(NT)
3.	Make copies	(NT)
4.	Compose meeting notes/agenda	(NT)
5.	Plan month-end (close) duties	(NT/T)
6.	Improve processes	(NT/T)
7.	File paper work	(NT/T)
8.	Route paper work	(NT)
9.	Compose policy/process documentation	(NT)
10.	Attend meetings	(NT)
11.	Schedule meetings	(NT)
12.	Find supporting documentation (pulling invoices)	(NT)
13.	Respond to written correspondence	(NT/T)
14.	Compose written correspondence	(NT/T)
15.	Complete expense reports	(NT/T)
16.	Track metrics	(NT/T)
17.	Attend 1 × 1's	(NT)
18.	Conduct 1 × 1's	(NT/T)
19.	Submit requests for materials/services	(NT)

Duty Area 2: Financial Analysis		
Task Number	**Task Statement**	**Formal (T) or Non-Formal Training (NT)**
1.	Review expense details	(NT/T)
2.	Identify variances prior to current period	(NT)
3.	Compare actuals to forecast	(T)
4.	Research reconciliations	(NT)
5.	Calculate rations to determine cause and effect (e.g. D80)	(T)
6.	Report root cause analysis of variance	(T)
7.	Research variances	(NT)
8.	Formulate conclusions	(T)
9.	Take corrective actions	(T)
10.	Use financial software to gather data	(T)
11.	Generate reports	(NT/T)
12.	Review financial analysis reports	(NT)
13.	Evaluate metrics	(T)
14.	Provide information to the financial analysts for forecasting	(T)
Duty Area 3: Core/Fundamentals		
Task Number	**Task Statement**	**Formal (T) or Non-Formal Training (NT)**
1.	New Hire Orientation	(T)
2.	Describe Dell Finance ethics policy	(T)
3.	State how the Dell Finance organization works	(T)
4.	Describe Dell's product lines (LOB)	(T)
5.	Use Dell terminology	(NT)
6.	State meaning of core accounting terms (e.g., balance sheet, income statement, general ledger, account reconciliation)	(NT)
7.	Describe the Dell close process	(NT)
8.	Describe Dell Financial software systems and inter-relationships	(T)
9.	Describe Dell and Dell Finance organizations	(NT)

Duty Area 4: Process Management		
*Note: Could possibly fit in with Finance New Hire		
Task Number	**Task Statement**	**Formal (T) or Non-Formal Training (NT)**
1.	Identify Finance processes	(T)
2.	State the internal controls for Finance	(T)
3.	Use internal controls	(T)
4.	Create data flow chart by organization (P&L and income statements by department)	(T)
5.	Make sure all close processes are completed as scheduled	(T)
6.	Describe the balance sheet review process (including players/participants)	(T)

Duty Area 5: Interpersonal Skills		
Task Number	**Task Statement**	**Formal (T) or Non-Formal Training (NT)**
1.	Exercise appropriate assertiveness	(T)
2.	Communicate ideas	(T)
3.	Make oral presentations	(T)
4.	Provide internal customer service	(NT)
5.	Determine people's learning styles/personality types	(T)
6.	Treat people professionally	(NT)
7.	Establish a good working relationship with manager	(NT)
8.	Resolve differences with peers or co-workers	(NT/T)
9.	Use proper tone/language for all written and voice mail communications	(T)
10.	Communicate with non-financial departments without using finance jargon.	(NT)

Duty Area 6: Problem Solving/Root Cause		
Task Number	**Task Statement**	**Formal (T) or Non-Formal Training (NT)**
1.	Establish system that identifies problems on a recurring basis	(NT/T)
2.	Define the problem	(T)
3.	Use software to research cause	(T)
4.	Identify financial impact of problem	(T)
5.	Determine who problem affects	(T)
6.	Conduct meeting with affected people	(T)
7.	Develop action plan	(T)

Task Number	Task Statement	Formal (T) or Non-Formal Training (NT)
	Duty Area 6: Problem Solving/Root Cause *(continued)*	
8.	Identify resources to implement	(T)
9.	Determine resolution	(T)
10.	Implement action plan/resolution	(T)
11.	Follow-up on resolution	
	Duty Area 7: Project Management	
1.	Attend project meetings	(NT)
2.	Determine action items/issues	(NT)
3.	Complete action items (to appropriate level)	(NT)
4.	Identify project objective	(NT)
5.	Identify client/sponsor	(NT)
6.	Ensure implementation	(NT)
7.	Act as a finance rep on various projects	(NT)
	Duty Area 8: Reconciliation Issue Analysis	
1.	Input data to DOMS and (ROSS) general ledger	(NT)
2.	Generate reconciliation schedule	(NT)
3.	Reconcile accounts manually	(NT)
4.	Conduct aging reports (flags for how long in system)	(NT)
5.	Identify reconciling items	(NT)
6.	Determine materiality for reconciling items	(NT)
7.	Research data for reconciliations	(NT)
8.	Use Hyperion/ROSS	(T)
9.	Determine corrective action	(NT)
10.	Take corrective action	(NT)

This sample task list shared by Sheila Wojick is being used as a self-assessment tool by the University Federal Credit Union in Austin, Texas for a loan processor position. Sheila, a trainer and facilitator, was able to use the JASR technique after a one-hour discussion. (Used with permission.)

Loan Processor
University Federal Credit Union

Job Task Self Assessment

5 = Expert
4 = Very Good
3 = Good
2 = Needs Occasional Assistance
1 = Almost Always Needs Assistance

Name: _____

Date: _____

TASKS	5	4	3	2	1	Comments
1. Basic Fundamentals						
Know Credit Union history						
Describe Credit Union philosophy						
Describe the organization of UFCU						
Know basic HR policies						
Submit accurate leave and time reports						
Describe all UFCU products and services						
Describe basic lending terminology						
State rates and terms						
Explain interest calculations						
Know basic Users Datasafe codes						
2. Processing						
Take an application, regardless of how submitted						
Fund a loan						
Close a loan—all types						

TASKS	5	4	3	2	1	Comments
2. *Processing* (continued)						
Process Skip-a-Payment, extensions, due date changes						
Post loan payments and reversals of all types, and back off late charges						
Verify employment						
Operate general ledger accounts						
File UCC1 Statements						
Post pay-off and mail out titles to proper party						
File all loan documents in loan file						
Process daily and monthly reports; update lines of credit						
Give drafting instructions						
Pay off a loan						
Open new accounts						
Process all lines of credit requests						
Process turn-down letter						
Explain payment histories						
Provide supporting information for title work						
3. *Administrative*						
File documents in loan folders						
Make copies						
Pick up and distribute mail						
Fax documents						
Type 25–30 wpm						
Use 10 key by touch						
Maintain files in document-order						
Maintain neat and clutter-free work area						
Attend meetings as required						
Order supplies						

TASKS	5	4	3	2	1	Comments
4. Communications						
Interact with co-workers and members by phone and in person in a professional and effective manner						
Use proper terminology, especially with members						
Use proper and consistent format for letters sent on Internet						
Practice patience in stressful situations						
Utilize effective conflict resolution and negotiation techniques						
Effectively explain decisions by loan officer to members						
Effectively explain variations in interest rates to members						
Be proficient in all written correspondence						
Practice good etiquette on phone						
5. Computer Skills						
Pull month-end reports using AE						
Pull extended account history using AE						
Compose and send e-mail						
Pull invoices and NADA values on PC						
Use LOS system						
Use all lending tran codes						
Pull Internet loan applications off system						
Create a document in Microsoft Word						
Customize form letters in Microsoft Word						

TASKS	5	4	3	2	1	Comments
6. Credit Analysis						
Use credit reports effectively						
Counsel members on credit improvement						
Calculate ratios used in LoanLine and be able to explain results of calculations to members						
Analyze ratios used in LoanLine and be able to explain to members						
Interpret financial statements and tax returns						
Verify income						
Analyze member profile						
Analyze application						
Understand Beacon scores and relevance to risk-based lending						
7. Problem Solving						
Determine facts before solving problems						
Research, locate, and solve problem						
Remain calm with members						
Accept exceptions						
Perform technical corrections						
Direct members to proper person or department						
Promote teamwork in problem solving						
Promote/communicate best problem-solving practices						
Remain open to creative solutions						
Use supervisor/manager to diffuse negative solutions						
Use empowerment to your advantage—know when to make a decision, and count on your manager's support						

TASKS	5	4	3	2	1	Comments
8. Financial Knowledge						
A. Be able to:						
Explain fundamentals of Truth In Lending						
Explain fundamentals of ECOA						
Explain fundamentals of RESPA						
Explain fundamentals of HMDA						
Explain fundamentals of Fair Credit Reporting Act						
Explain fundamentals of Texas Homestead Law						
Explain fundamentals of tax returns and financial statements						
Explain fundamentals of bankruptcy procedures						
Explain fundamentals of 1st Lien RE procedures						
Explain fundamentals of FNMA underwriting guidelines						
Explain fundamentals of all UFCU lending documents						
B. Be able to:						
Comply with Truth In Lending						
Comply with ECOA						
Comply with RESPA						
Comply with HMDA						
Comply with the Fair Credit Reporting Act						
Comply with the Texas Homestead Law						
Comply with 1st Lien RE procedures						
Comply with FNMA underwriting guidelines						
Comply with all UFCU lending documents						
C. Explain fundamentals of escalation policy for problem resolution and decision making						

TASKS	5	4	3	2	1	Comments
9. Member Service						
Cross-sell UFCU products and services						
Be professional and courteous						
Listen to members (and co-workers)						
Explain how credit union services will benefit members						
Treat members as you would desire to be treated						
Transmit positive image to members over phone and in person—*smile*						
Accurately answer any loan-related questions						

Glossary of Terms *and* Acronym List

Behavioral Event Interview—A data collection technique, based on the Critical Incident Technique, that uses specially structured interviews of superior and average performers to piece together commonality in job performance. David McClelland originally created this process.

Competency—"Competencies are underlying characteristics of people and indicate ways of behaving or thinking, generalizing across situations, and enduring for a reasonably long period of time." (Spencer, p. 9)

Configured Work—"Work that is defined and designed in place, in response to the situation at hand, and by the person(s) doing it." (Nickols) *See "prefigured work."*

Critical Incident Technique—A technique that consists of a set of procedures for collecting direct observations of human behavior to facilitate their potential usefulness in solving practical problems and developing broad psychological principles. (Zemke, p. 277)

DACUM—"Developing A Curriculum" job analysis method

Duty Area—Grouping of similar tasks. For example, there might be a duty area for "Administration" or "Problem Solving" or "Communication."

Exemplars—High performers in a job position

Formal Training—Training that uses structured classroom instruction, structured on-the-job training, computer-based training, self-paced training, or other training that uses structured methods in the delivery.

JASR—Acronym for "Job Analysis at the Speed of Reality"

Job—"A collection of related activities, duties, or responsibilities." (Rothwell, p. 118)

Job Analysis—A systematic examination of what people do, how they do it, and what results they achieve by doing it. (Rothwell, p. 118)

Knowledge Worker—Workers who have information and knowledge as both the raw material of their labor and its product. (Stewart, p. 41)

Listserv—A family of programs that automatically manage mailing lists—distributing messages posted to the list, adding or deleting members, and so on without manual involvement. The names of mailing lists maintained by LISTSERV usually end with—l. (Levine and Baroudi, p. 387)

Non-Formal Training—Any training method, tool, or intervention that is not structured in nature. Examples of this include use of simple job aids and just-in-time coaching.

Performance Test—A test that uses objective-based criteria to determine whether or not an individual can perform the desired task. Conditions and standards for the performance must be clearly identified and validated prior to implementing the performance test. Participants (or students) who take a performance test already have seen the learning objectives prior to an actual performance test.

Prefigured work—"Work that has been defined and designed in advance, for execution under a set of well-defined standard conditions. Prefigured work is usually defined and designed by someone other than the person who will be expected to accomplish it." (Fred Nickols) *See configured work.*

SME—Subject Matter Expert

Task—"A discrete unit of work performed by an individual. It usually combines a logical and necessary step in the performance of a job duty, and typically has an identifiable beginning and ending." (Rothwell, p. 125)

Validated Task List—A list that hierarchically breaks a job down into its component duty or functional areas and tasks. The task list is validated because exemplar job incumbents and managers are involved in the process.

Job Analysis Internet Resources

Compiled here is a list of various Internet and web-related sites that you may find interesting as you look for additional information on job analysis and related topics in the field. Due to the dynamic nature of web sites, it is possible that some of the web sites will change names or servers. I've provided enough here to get you started.

http://train.ed.psu.edu/trdev-l/—This is a web site that describes the Training and Development Listserv. This Listserv is used by thousands of trainers, training managers, performance consultants, instructional designers, etc. from around the world who are interested in keeping current with the latest trends in the industry. This is a great place to pose those tough questions you need answered.

http://www.ijoa.org/—Web site for the Institute for Job and Occupational Analysis (IJOA). The IJOA is a not-for-profit educational and scientific corporation that focuses on new technologies for assessing jobs and occupations.

http://harvey.psyc.vt.edu/jamailinglist.html—This is where you will find out how to subscribe to the Job Analysis Listserv.

http://www.uscg.mil/hq/g-w/g-wt/g-wtt/g-wtt-1/oasite/recent.htm—If you'd like to see some recent job analyses conducted by the Coast Guard, go here. The Coasts Guard and other military organizations really get into job analysis, and at a very deep level. Some of the reports in these files are over 30 pages long. If you don't have it already, you'll want to install the Adobe Acrobat Reader. (Go to http://www.adobe.com)

http://www.hrsit.com/index.htm—Another site that describes why and how job analysis is done.

http://www.claytonwallis.com/cxomf.htm—Integrated job and competency analysis software.

http://www.aimmconsult.com/JAreference.html—Why Should I Conduct Job Analysis? This site posts information regarding reasons for conducting job analyses.

http://home.navisoft.com/hrmbasics/jobs.htm—A job analysis link page with multiple job analysis web sites.

http://www.nocti.org/—A web site for the National Occupational Competency Testing Institute. The National Occupational Competency Testing Institute (NOCTI) is the nation's foremost provider of occupational competency assessments to education, business, industry, government, and the military. The NOCTI offers over 150 different technical tests that have been nationally validated to reflect entry level and experienced worker skills. NOCTI's tests are carefully constructed by skilled technicians, career and technical educators, and test development specialists from across the nation. They are continually reviewed and updated to reflect new technologies, job titles, and national standards.

http://www.codap.com/—The Sensible Systems, Inc. (SSI) mission is to promote the long-term spread of responsible and sustainable job and occupational analysis (OA) methodologies and technologies. This web site describes the company's product for job analysis.

http://www.interlynx.net/archway/ohio/Connecti.htm—The DACUM Connection. This site is dedicated to DACUM.

References

Bemis, Stephen E., Belenky, Ann Holt, and Soder, Dee Ann. *Job Analysis: An Effective Management Tool.* (1983). Washington, D.C.: The Bureau of National Affairs, Inc.

Davis, Stan and Meyer, Christopher. *Blur.* (1998). Reading, Massachusetts: Addison-Wesley Publishing Company.

Higgins, James M. *101 Creative Problem Solving Techniques.* (1994). Winter Park, Florida: The New Management Publishing Company.

Levine, John R. and Baroudi, Carol. *The Internet for Dummies.* (1994). San Mateo: IDG Books Worldwide, Inc.

Nickols, Fred. *The Autonomous Performer: Implications for Performance Technology.* (1997). Unpublished manuscript presented at Dell University.

Norton, Robert. *DACUM.* (1985). Center on Education and Training for Employment; Ohio State University.

Rothwell, William J. and Kazanas, H. C. *Mastering the Instructional Design Process.* (1998). San Francisco: Jossey-Bass.

Spencer, Lyle M. and Spencer, Signe M. *Competence at Work.* (1993). New York: John Wiley & Sons, Inc.

Stewart, Thomas A. *Intellectual Capital.* (1997). New York: Doubleday.

Zemke, Ron and Kramlinger, Thomas. *Figuring Things Out: A Trainer's Guide to Needs and Task Analysis.* (1982). Reading, Massachusetts: Addison-Wesley Publishing Company.

About the Author

Darin Hartley has been working in the training industry for the past ten years and has undergraduate and graduate degrees in Corporate Training and Training Management. He is the Program Manager of the Dell Learning Technology Services Department of Dell Computer Corporation's training organization, Dell University. Darin has presented previously at ISPI International, ASTD International, and the ASTD Technical Skills Training Conference on the topic. He has authored articles for *Technical & Skills Training* and *WorkForce* Magazines.

Prior to Dell, Darin has worked for Lockheed Martin, EG&G, General Physics Corporation, and the US Navy as a nuclear power plant operator (eight years). He currently resides in Pflugerville, Texas just north of Austin.

Darin can be reached via e-mail at:

DHartley@texas.net
or
Darin_Hartley@Dell.com.

Job Analysis and Performance Management

Course Calendar

Class	Text/Reading/Class Content
1.	Introduction of course, overview of material
2.	Hartley, pp. 1-22
	Job Analysis assignments for class projects
3.	Hartley, pp. 21-41
4.	Hartley, pp. 41-55
5.	Hartley, pp. 55-108
6.	Hartley, pp. 55-108
7.	Job Analysis projects DUE
8.	Daniels pp. 1 20
9.	Daniels pp. 21 50
10.	Daniels pp. 51 89
11.	Daniels pp. 90 - 115
12.	Daniels pp. 116 - 141
13.	Daniels pp. 142 - 178
14.	Daniels pp. 179 - 197
15.	Daniels pp. 198 - 231

Other Readings

APS Observer, (1992). Human Capital Initiative, Report of the National Behavioral Science Research Agenda Committee. February.

APS Observer, (1993). Human Capital Initiative, the Changing Nature of Work. October.

Bjork, R. & Druckman D. (1991). How do you improve human performance. *APS Observer*, Nov. 13- 15.

Dweck, C.S. (1992). The study of goals in psychology. *Psychological Science*, 3, 3, 165-167.

Deci, E.L. (1992). On the nature and functions of motivation theories. *Psychological Science*, 3, 3, 167-171.

----- (1991). What can monkey factors tell us about human factors? *APS Observer*, Nov. p.5.

Gordon, G.G. (1991). Industry determinants of organizational culture. *Academy of Management Review*. 16, 2, 396-415.

Medin, D.L., Goldstone, R.L., & Gentner, D. (1990). Similarity involving attributes and relations: judgments of similarities and difference are not inverses. *Psychological Science*, 1, 1, 64-69.

Platt, J.R. (1964). Strong inference. *Science,* 146, 85-98.

Wygonik, E.J. (1985). Analyzing office automation. *Topics in Health Records Management*, 6 (2) 12-21.

Job Analysis and Performance Management

Web Sites of Interest to Job Analysis

These are listed on the SIOP gateway, *SIOP IO Related Pages on the WWW* page. Address is www.siop.org/iorelatedpages.html. Some of the more interesting ones related to job analysis are:

Havey's Job Analysis and Personality Research @ harvey.psyyc.vt.edu/
Institute for Work Psychology
HRGuide @ hr.guide.com/jobanal
Dictionary of Occupational Titles @ oalj.dol.gov/libdot.htm
University of South Queens at http://www.usq.edu.au/ancil/fos/69373/links.htm
ccnet.com/^bluenote
International Assessment Network @ www.11209.134.156.100/excite/AT-DOTquery.htm
One Net @onetcenter.org

Companies that specialize in job analysis with interesting sites

Alderwick Consulting @ alderwick-consulting.co.uk/
Analysis Group   @theanalysisgroup.com
Clayton Wallis   @claytonwallis.com
HRTools   @hrtools.com
PAQ   @Paq.com

If you find any other interesting job analysis related sites, let me know and I'll include them.

Job Analysis and Performance Management

Edward J. Wygonik, Ph.D.
Associate Professor

Office.   Downtown Campus
Office Hours: Mondays, 3:00-5:00 or by appointment
Telephone: 312.341.3760

Robin Campus
Office Hours: Tuesdays, 3:00-5:00 or by appointment
Telephone: 312.341.3760

Email: Wygoniked @AOL.com

Course.   Psychology 664
Job Analysis and Performance Management
3 semester hour credit course

Description. This course is divided into two major sections, Job Analysis and Performance Management. In Job Analysis, information regarding the theories and techniques used in analyzing and classifying positions is presented. In Performance Management, students look at models and methods for improving employee performance.

Required Texts.

Hartley, D. (1999), *Job analysis at the speed of reality*. HRD PRess, Amherst, Ma.

Daniels, A.C. *Performance management*. Performance Management Publications, Tucker, Ga.

Other readings will be on reserve in the library and announced in class.

Course Requirements

- Read texts and articles on reserve
- Conduct a Job Analysis
- Conduct a Performance Management analysis

Job Analysis and Performance Management

Edward J. Wygonik, Ph.D.
Associate Professor

Office.   Downtown Campus
Office Hours: Mondays, 3:00-5:00 or by appointment
Telephone: 312.341.3760

Robin Campus
Office Hours: Tuesdays, 3:00-5:00 or by appointment
Telephone: 312.341.3760

Email: Wygoniked @AOL.com

Course.   Psychology 664
Job Analysis and Performance Management
3 semester hour credit course

Description. This course is divided into two major sections, Job Analysis and Performance Management. In Job Analysis, information regarding the theories and techniques used in analyzing and classifying positions is presented. In Performance Management, students look at models and methods for improving employee performance.

Required Texts.

Hartley, D. (1999), *Job analysis at the speed of reality*. HRD PRess, Amherst, Ma.

Daniels, A.C. *Performance management*. Performance Management Publications, Tucker, Ga.

Other readings will be on reserve in the library and announced in class.

Course Requirements

- Read texts and articles on reserve
- Conduct a Job Analysis
- Conduct a Performance Management analysis

The above schedule and procedures in this course are subject to change in the event of extenuating circumstances.
0101

Job Analysis and Performance Management

Edward J. Wygonik, Ph.D.
Associate Professor

Office.   Downtown Campus
              Office Hours: Mondays, 3:00-5:00 or by appointment
              Telephone: 312.341.3760

              Robin Campus
              Office Hours: Tuesdays, 3:00-5:00 or by appointment
              Telephone: 312.341.3760

              Email: Wygoniked @AOL.com

Course.   Psychology 664
              Job Analysis and Performance Management
              3 semester hour credit course

Description. This course is divided into two major sections, Job Analysis and Performance Management. In Job Analysis, information regarding the theories and techniques used in analyzing and classifying positions is presented. In Performance Management, students look at models and methods for improving employee performance.

Required Texts.

Hartley, D. (1999), *Job analysis at the speed of reality*. HRD PRess, Amherst, Ma.

Daniels, A.C. *Performance management*. Performance Management Publications, Tucker, Ga.

Other readings will be on reserve in the library and announced in class.

Course Requirements

- Read texts and articles on reserve
- Conduct a Job Analysis
- Conduct a Performance Management analysis

The above schedule and procedures in this course are subject to change in the event of extenuating circumstances.
0101

Job Analysis and Performance Management

Web Sites of Interest to Job Analysis

These are listed on the SIOP gateway, *SIOP IO Related Pages on the WWW* page. Address is www.siop.org/iorelatedpages.html. Some of the more interesting ones related to job analysis are:

Havey's Job Analysis and Personality Research @ harvey.psyyc.vt.edu/
Institute for Work Psychology
HRGuide @ hr.guide.com/jobanal
Dictionary of Occupational Titles @ oalj.dol.gov/libdot.htm
University of South Queens at http://www.usq.edu.au/ancil/fos/69373/links.htm
ccnet.com/^bluenote
International Assessment Network @ www.11209.134.156.100/excite/AT-DOTquery.htm
One Net @onetcenter.org

Companies that specialize in job analysis with interesting sites

Alderwick Consulting @ alderwick-consulting.co.uk/
Analysis Group   @theanalysisgroup.com
Clayton Wallis   @claytonwallis.com
HRTools   @hrtools.com
PAQ   @Paq.com

If you find any other interesting job analysis related sites, let me know and I'll include them.

Job Analysis and Performance Management

Course Calendar

Class	Text/Reading/Class Content
1.	Introduction of course, overview of material
2.	Hartley, pp. 1-22
	Job Analysis assignments for class projects
3.	Hartley, pp. 21-41
4.	Hartley, pp. 41-55
5.	Hartley, pp. 55-108
6.	Hartley, pp. 55-108
7.	Job Analysis projects DUE
8.	Daniels pp. 1 20
9.	Daniels pp. 21 50
10.	Daniels pp. 51 89
11.	Daniels pp. 90 - 115
12.	Daniels pp. 116 - 141
13.	Daniels pp. 142 - 178
14.	Daniels pp. 179 - 197
15.	Daniels pp. 198 - 231

Other Readings

APS Observer, (1992). Human Capital Initiative, Report of the National Behavioral Science Research Agenda Committee. February.

APS Observer, (1993). Human Capital Initiative, the Changing Nature of Work. October.

Bjork, R. & Druckman D. (1991). How do you improve human performance. *APS Observer*, Nov. 13- 15.

Dweck, C.S. (1992). The study of goals in psychology. *Psychological Science*, 3, 3, 165-167.

Deci, E.L. (1992). On the nature and functions of motivation theories. *Psychological Science*, 3, 3, 167-171.

----- (1991). What can monkey factors tell us about human factors? *APS Observer*, Nov. p.5.

Gordon, G.G. (1991). Industry determinants of organizational culture. *Academy of Management Review*. 16, 2, 396-415.

Medin, D.L., Goldstone, R.L., & Gentner, D. (1990). Similarity involving attributes and relations: judgments of similarities and difference are not inverses. *Psychological Science*, 1, 1, 64-69.

Platt, J.R. (1964). Strong inference. *Science*, 146, 85-98.

Wygonik, E.J. (1985). Analyzing office automation. *Topics in Health Records Management*, 6 (2) 12-21.

Job Analysis and Performance Management

Course Calendar

Class	Text/Reading/Class Content
1.	Introduction of course, overview of material
2.	Hartley, pp. 1-22
	Job Analysis assignments for class projects
3.	Hartley, pp. 21-41
4.	Hartley, pp. 41-55
5.	Hartley, pp. 55-108
6.	Hartley, pp. 55-108
7.	Job Analysis projects DUE
8.	Daniels pp. 1 20
9.	Daniels pp. 21 50
10.	Daniels pp. 51 89
11.	Daniels pp. 90 - 115
12.	Daniels pp. 116 - 141
13.	Daniels pp. 142 - 178
14.	Daniels pp. 179 - 197
15.	Daniels pp. 198 - 231

Other Readings

APS Observer, (1992). Human Capital Initiative, Report of the National Behavioral Science Research Agenda Committee. February.

APS Observer, (1993). Human Capital Initiative, the Changing Nature of Work. October.

Bjork, R. & Druckman D. (1991). How do you improve human performance. *APS Observer*, Nov. 13- 15.

Dweck, C.S. (1992). The study of goals in psychology. *Psychological Science*, 3, 3, 165-167.

Deci, E.L. (1992). On the nature and functions of motivation theories. *Psychological Science*, 3, 3, 167-171.

----- (1991). What can monkey factors tell us about human factors? *APS Observer*, Nov. p.5.

Gordon, G.G. (1991). Industry determinants of organizational culture. *Academy of Management Review*. 16, 2, 396-415.

Medin, D.L., Goldstone, R.L., & Gentner, D. (1990). Similarity involving attributes and relations: judgments of similarities and difference are not inverses. *Psychological Science*, 1, 1, 64-69.

Platt, J.R. (1964). Strong inference. *Science,* 146, 85-98.

Wygonik, E.J. (1985). Analyzing office automation. *Topics in Health Records Management*, 6 (2) 12-21.

The above schedule and procedures in this course are subject to change in the event of extenuating circumstances.
0101

Job Analysis and Performance Management

Web Sites of Interest to Job Analysis

These are listed on the SIOP gateway, *SIOP IO Related Pages on the WWW* page. Address is www.siop.org/iorelatedpages.html. Some of the more interesting ones related to job analysis are:

Havey's Job Analysis and Personality Research @ harvey.psyyc.vt.edu/
Institute for Work Psychology
HRGuide @ hr.guide.com/jobanal
Dictionary of Occupational Titles @ oalj.dol.gov/libdot.htm
University of South Queens at http://www.usq.edu.au/ancil/fos/69373/links.htm
ccnet.com/^bluenote
International Assessment Network @ www.11209.134.156.100/excite/AT-DOTquery.htm
One Net @onetcenter.org

Companies that specialize in job analysis with interesting sites

Alderwick Consulting @ alderwick-consulting.co.uk/
Analysis Group   @theanalysisgroup.com
Clayton Wallis   @claytonwallis.com
HRTools   @hrtools.com
PAQ   @Paq.com

If you find any other interesting job analysis related sites, let me know and I'll include them.

Job Analysis and Performance Management

Edward J. Wygonik, Ph.D.
Associate Professor

Office.   Downtown Campus
             Office Hours: Mondays, 3:00-5:00 or by appointment
             Telephone: 312.341.3760

             Robin Campus
             Office Hours: Tuesdays, 3:00-5:00 or by appointment
             Telephone: 312.341.3760

             Email: Wygoniked @AOL.com

Course.   Psychology 664
             Job Analysis and Performance Management
             3 semester hour credit course

Description. This course is divided into two major sections, Job Analysis and Performance Management. In Job Analysis, information regarding the theories and techniques used in analyzing and classifying positions is presented. In Performance Management, students look at models and methods for improving employee performance.

Required Texts.

Hartley, D. (1999), *Job analysis at the speed of reality*. HRD PRess, Amherst, Ma.

Daniels, A.C. *Performance management*. Performance Management Publications, Tucker, Ga.

Other readings will be on reserve in the library and announced in class.

Course Requirements

- Read texts and articles on reserve
- Conduct a Job Analysis
- Conduct a Performance Management analysis

The above schedule and procedures in this course are subject to change in the event of extenuating circumstances.
0101

Job Analysis and Performance Management

Course Calendar

Class	Text/Reading/Class Content
1.	Introduction of course, overview of material
2.	Hartley, pp. 1-22
	Job Analysis assignments for class projects
3.	Hartley, pp. 21-41
4.	Hartley, pp. 41-55
5.	Hartley, pp. 55-108
6.	Hartley, pp. 55-108
7.	Job Analysis projects DUE
8.	Daniels pp. 1 20
9.	Daniels pp. 21 50
10.	Daniels pp. 51 89
11.	Daniels pp. 90 - 115
12.	Daniels pp. 116 - 141
13.	Daniels pp. 142 - 178
14.	Daniels pp. 179 - 197
15.	Daniels pp. 198 - 231

Other Readings

APS Observer, (1992). Human Capital Initiative, Report of the National Behavioral Science Research Agenda Committee. February.

APS Observer, (1993). Human Capital Initiative, the Changing Nature of Work. October.

Bjork, R. & Druckman D. (1991). How do you improve human performance. *APS Observer*, Nov. 13- 15.

Dweck, C.S. (1992). The study of goals in psychology. *Psychological Science*, 3, 3, 165-167.

Deci, E.L. (1992). On the nature and functions of motivation theories. *Psychological Science*, 3, 3, 167-171.

----- (1991). What can monkey factors tell us about human factors? *APS Observer*, Nov. p.5.

Gordon, G.G. (1991). Industry determinants of organizational culture. *Academy of Management Review*. 16, 2, 396-415.

Medin, D.L., Goldstone, R.L., & Gentner, D. (1990). Similarity involving attributes and relations: judgments of similarities and difference are not inverses. *Psychological Science*, 1, 1, 64-69.

Platt, J.R. (1964). Strong inference. *Science*, 146, 85-98.

Wygonik, E.J. (1985). Analyzing office automation. *Topics in Health Records Management*, 6 (2) 12-21.

The above schedule and procedures in this course are subject to change in the event of extenuating circumstances.

Job Analysis and Performance Management

Web Sites of Interest to Job Analysis

These are listed on the SIOP gateway, *SIOP IO Related Pages on the WWW* page. Address is www.siop.org/iorelatedpages.html. Some of the more interesting ones related to job analysis are:

Havey's Job Analysis and Personality Research @ harvey.psyyc.vt.edu/
Institute for Work Psychology
HRGuide @ hr.guide.com/jobanal
Dictionary of Occupational Titles @ oalj.dol.gov/libdot.htm
University of South Queens at http://www.usq.edu.au/ancil/fos/69373/links.htm
ccnet.com/^bluenote
International Assessment Network @ www.11209.134.156.100/excite/AT-DOTquery.htm
One Net @onetcenter.org

Companies that specialize in job analysis with interesting sites

Alderwick Consulting @ alderwick-consulting.co.uk/
Analysis Group   @theanalysisgroup.com
Clayton Wallis   @claytonwallis.com
HRTools   @hrtools.com
PAQ   @Paq.com

If you find any other interesting job analysis related sites, let me know and I'll include them.

Job Analysis and Performance Management

Edward J. Wygonik, Ph.D.
Associate Professor

Office.   Downtown Campus
Office Hours: Mondays, 3:00-5:00 or by appointment
Telephone: 312.341.3760

Robin Campus
Office Hours: Tuesdays, 3:00-5:00 or by appointment
Telephone: 312.341.3760

Email: Wygoniked @AOL.com

Course.   Psychology 664
Job Analysis and Performance Management
3 semester hour credit course

Description. This course is divided into two major sections, Job Analysis and Performance Management. In Job Analysis, information regarding the theories and techniques used in analyzing and classifying positions is presented. In Performance Management, students look at models and methods for improving employee performance.

Required Texts.

Hartley, D. (1999), *Job analysis at the speed of reality*. HRD PRess, Amherst, Ma.

Daniels, A.C. *Performance management*. Performance Management Publications, Tucker, Ga.

Other readings will be on reserve in the library and announced in class.

Course Requirements

- Read texts and articles on reserve
- Conduct a Job Analysis
- Conduct a Performance Management analysis

The above schedule and procedures in this course are subject to change in the event of extenuating circumstances.
0101

Job Analysis and Performance Management

Course Calendar

Class	Text/Reading/Class Content
1.	Introduction of course, overview of material
2.	Hartley, pp. 1-22
	Job Analysis assignments for class projects
3.	Hartley, pp. 21-41
4.	Hartley, pp. 41-55
5.	Hartley, pp. 55-108
6.	Hartley, pp. 55-108
7.	Job Analysis projects DUE
8.	Daniels pp. 1 20
9.	Daniels pp. 21 50
10.	Daniels pp. 51 89
11.	Daniels pp. 90 - 115
12.	Daniels pp. 116 - 141
13.	Daniels pp. 142 - 178
14.	Daniels pp. 179 - 197
15.	Daniels pp. 198 - 231

Other Readings

APS Observer, (1992). Human Capital Initiative, Report of the National Behavioral Science Research Agenda Committee. February.

APS Observer, (1993). Human Capital Initiative, the Changing Nature of Work. October.

Bjork, R. & Druckman D. (1991). How do you improve human performance. *APS Observer*, Nov. 13- 15.

Dweck, C.S. (1992). The study of goals in psychology. *Psychological Science*, 3, 3, 165-167.

Deci, E.L. (1992). On the nature and functions of motivation theories. *Psychological Science*, 3, 3, 167-171.

----- (1991). What can monkey factors tell us about human factors? *APS Observer*, Nov. p.5.

Gordon, G.G. (1991). Industry determinants of organizational culture. *Academy of Management Review*. 16, 2, 396-415.

Medin, D.L., Goldstone, R.L., & Gentner, D. (1990). Similarity involving attributes and relations: judgments of similarities and difference are not inverses. *Psychological Science*, 1, 1, 64-69.

Platt, J.R. (1964). Strong inference. *Science*, 146, 85-98.

Wygonik, E.J. (1985). Analyzing office automation. *Topics in Health Records Management*, 6 (2) 12-21.

Job Analysis and Performance Management

Web Sites of Interest to Job Analysis

These are listed on the SIOP gateway, *SIOP IO Related Pages on the WWW* page. Address is www.siop.org/iorelatedpages.html.   Some of the more interesting ones related to job analysis are:

Havey's Job Analysis and Personality Research @ harvey.psyyc.vt.edu/
Institute for Work Psychology
HRGuide @ hr.guide.com/jobanal
Dictionary of Occupational Titles @ oalj.dol.gov/libdot.htm
University of South Queens at http://www.usq.edu.au/ancil/fos/69373/links.htm
ccnet.com/^bluenote
International Assessment Network @ www.11209.134.156.100/excite/AT-DOTquery.htm
One Net @onetcenter.org

Companies that specialize in job analysis with interesting sites

Alderwick Consulting @ alderwick-consulting.co.uk/
Analysis Group   @theanalysisgroup.com
Clayton Wallis   @claytonwallis.com
HRTools   @hrtools.com
PAQ   @Paq.com

If you find any other interesting job analysis related sites, let me know and I'll include them.

The above schedule and procedures in this course are subject to change in the event of extenuating circumstances.
0101

Job Analysis and Performance Management

Edward J. Wygonik, Ph.D.
Associate Professor

Office.　　Downtown Campus
　　　　　　Office Hours: Mondays, 3:00-5:00 or by appointment
　　　　　　Telephone:　312.341.3760

　　　　　　Robin Campus
　　　　　　Office Hours: Tuesdays, 3:00-5:00 or by appointment
　　　　　　Telephone:　312.341.3760

　　　　　　Email: Wygoniked @AOL.com

Course.　　Psychology 664
　　　　　　Job Analysis and Performance Management
　　　　　　3 semester hour credit course

Description. This course is divided into two major sections, Job Analysis and Performance Management. In Job Analysis, information regarding the theories and techniques used in analyzing and classifying positions is presented. In Performance Management, students look at models and methods for improving employee performance.

Required Texts.

Hartley, D. (1999), *Job analysis at the speed of reality*. HRD PRess, Amherst, Ma.

Daniels, A.C. *Performance management*. Performance Management Publications, Tucker, Ga.

Other readings will be on reserve in the library and announced in class.

Course Requirements

- Read texts and articles on reserve
- Conduct a Job Analysis
- Conduct a Performance Management analysis

Job Analysis and Performance Management

Course Calendar

Class	Text/Reading/Class Content
1.	Introduction of course, overview of material
2.	Hartley, pp. 1-22
	Job Analysis assignments for class projects
3.	Hartley, pp. 21-41
4.	Hartley, pp. 41-55
5.	Hartley, pp. 55-108
6.	Hartley, pp. 55-108
7.	Job Analysis projects DUE
8.	Daniels pp. 1 20
9.	Daniels pp. 21 50
10.	Daniels pp. 51 89
11.	Daniels pp. 90 - 115
12.	Daniels pp. 116 - 141
13.	Daniels pp. 142 - 178
14.	Daniels pp. 179 - 197
15.	Daniels pp. 198 - 231

Other Readings

APS Observer, (1992). Human Capital Initiative, Report of the National Behavioral Science Research Agenda Committee. February.

APS Observer, (1993). Human Capital Initiative, the Changing Nature of Work. October.

Bjork, R. & Druckman D. (1991). How do you improve human performance. *APS Observer*, Nov. 13- 15.

Dweck, C.S. (1992). The study of goals in psychology. *Psychological Science*, 3, 3, 165-167.

Deci, E.L. (1992). On the nature and functions of motivation theories. *Psychological Science*, 3, 3, 167-171.

----- (1991). What can monkey factors tell us about human factors? *APS Observer*, Nov. p.5.

Gordon, G.G. (1991). Industry determinants of organizational culture. *Academy of Management Review*. 16, 2, 396-415.

Medin, D.L., Goldstone, R.L., & Gentner, D. (1990). Similarity involving attributes and relations: judgments of similarities and difference are not inverses. *Psychological Science*, 1, 1, 64-69.

Platt, J.R. (1964). Strong inference. *Science*, 146, 85-98.

Wygonik, E.J. (1985). Analyzing office automation. *Topics in Health Records Management*, 6 (2) 12-21.

The above schedule and procedures in this course are subject to change in the event of extenuating circumstances.
0101

Job Analysis and Performance Management

Web Sites of Interest to Job Analysis

These are listed on the SIOP gateway, *SIOP IO Related Pages on the WWW* page. Address is www.siop.org/iorelatedpages.html.   Some of the more interesting ones related to job analysis are:

Havey's Job Analysis and Personality Research @ harvey.psyyc.vt.edu/
Institute for Work Psychology
HRGuide @ hr.guide.com/jobanal
Dictionary of Occupational Titles @ oalj.dol.gov/libdot.htm
University of South Queens at http://www.usq.edu.au/ancil/fos/69373/links.htm
ccnet.com/^bluenote
International Assessment Network @ www.11209.134.156.100/excite/AT-DOTquery.htm
One Net @onetcenter.org

Companies that specialize in job analysis with interesting sites

Alderwick Consulting @ alderwick-consulting.co.uk/
Analysis Group   @theanalysisgroup.com
Clayton Wallis   @claytonwallis.com
HRTools   @hrtools.com
PAQ   @Paq.com

If you find any other interesting job analysis related sites, let me know and I'll include them.

Job Analysis and Performance Management

Edward J. Wygonik, Ph.D.
Associate Professor

Office.   Downtown Campus
Office Hours: Mondays, 3:00-5:00 or by appointment
Telephone: 312.341.3760

Robin Campus
Office Hours: Tuesdays, 3:00-5:00 or by appointment
Telephone: 312.341.3760

Email: Wygoniked @AOL.com

Course.   Psychology 664
Job Analysis and Performance Management
3 semester hour credit course

Description. This course is divided into two major sections, Job Analysis and Performance Management. In Job Analysis, information regarding the theories and techniques used in analyzing and classifying positions is presented. In Performance Management, students look at models and methods for improving employee performance.

Required Texts.

Hartley, D. (1999), *Job analysis at the speed of reality*. HRD PRess, Amherst, Ma.

Daniels, A.C. *Performance management*. Performance Management Publications, Tucker, Ga.

Other readings will be on reserve in the library and announced in class.

Course Requirements

- Read texts and articles on reserve
- Conduct a Job Analysis
- Conduct a Performance Management analysis

The above schedule and procedures in this course are subject to change in the event of extenuating circumstances.
0101

Job Analysis and Performance Management

Course Calendar

Class   **Text/Reading/Class Content**

1. *V22*   Introduction of course, overview of material
2. *1/29*   Hartley, pp. 1-22
             Job Analysis assignments for class projects
3. *2/5*   Hartley, pp. 21-41
4. *2/12*   Hartley, pp. 41-55
5. *2/19*   Hartley, pp. 55-108
6. *2/26*   Hartley, pp. 55-108
7. *—*   Job Analysis projects DUE
8.   Daniels pp. 1 20
9.   Daniels pp. 21 50
10.   Daniels pp. 51 89
11.   Daniels pp. 90 - 115
12.   Daniels pp. 116 - 141
13.   Daniels pp. 142 - 178
14.   Daniels pp. 179 - 197
15.   Daniels pp. 198 - 231

Other Readings

APS Observer, (1992). Human Capital Initiative, Report of the National Behavioral Science Research Agenda Committee. February.

APS Observer, (1993). Human Capital Initiative, the Changing Nature of Work. October.

Bjork, R. & Druckman D. (1991). How do you improve human performance. *APS Observer*, Nov. 13- 15.

Dweck, C.S. (1992). The study of goals in psychology. *Psychological Science*, 3, 3, 165-167.

Deci, E.L. (1992). On the nature and functions of motivation theories. *Psychological Science*, 3, 3, 167-171.

----- (1991). What can monkey factors tell us about human factors? *APS Observer*, Nov. p.5.

Gordon, G.G. (1991). Industry determinants of organizational culture. *Academy of Management Review.* 16, 2, 396-415.

Medin, D.L., Goldstone, R.L., & Gentner, D. (1990). Similarity involving attributes and relations: judgments of similarities and difference are not inverses. *Psychological Science*, 1, 1, 64-69.

Platt, J.R. (1964). Strong inference. *Science,* 146, 85-98.

Wygonik, E.J. (1985). Analyzing office automation. *Topics in Health Records Management*, 6 (2) 12-21.

The above schedule and procedures in this course are subject to change in the event of extenuating circumstances.
0101

Job Analysis and Performance Management

Web Sites of Interest to Job Analysis

These are listed on the SIOP gateway, *SIOP IO Related Pages on the WWW* page. Address is www.siop.org/iorelatedpages.html. Some of the more interesting ones related to job analysis are:

Havey's Job Analysis and Personality Research @ harvey.psyyc.vt.edu/
Institute for Work Psychology
HRGuide @ hr.guide.com/jobanal
Dictionary of Occupational Titles @ oalj.dol.gov/libdot.htm
University of South Queens at http://www.usq.edu.au/ancil/fos/69373/links.htm
ccnet.com/^bluenote
International Assessment Network @ www.11209.134.156.100/excite/AT-DOTquery.htm
One Net @onetcenter.org

Companies that specialize in job analysis with interesting sites

Alderwick Consulting @ alderwick-consulting.co.uk/
Analysis Group   @theanalysisgroup.com
Clayton Wallis   @claytonwallis.com
HRTools   @hrtools.com
PAQ   @Paq.com

If you find any other interesting job analysis related sites, let me know and I'll include them.